Best in the Nation

Best in the Nation

The First Two Hundred Years of Ohio Libraries

EDITED BY **Melinda F. Hill**

The Wooster Book Company
Wooster Ohio ∽ 2003

The Wooster Book Company
205 West Liberty Street
Wooster, Ohio 44691
www.woosterbook.com
800-WUBOOK-1 • (800-982-6651)

Copyright © 2003 OHIO LIBRARY COUNCIL

All rights reserved.
No part of this book may be reproduced or utilized in any form or by any means, electronic or mechanical, including photocopying and recording, or by any information storage and retrieval system, without permission in writing from the publisher.
Published in the United States of America.

ISBN: 1-59098-660-1

Cover photo: B. Miller, *Wish I Was There Photography,* Delaware Ohio
Bookplate art: Jesse R. Ewing, Creston Ohio

Library of Congress Cataloging-in-Publication Data

Best in the nation : the first two hundred years of Ohio libraries / edited by Melinda F. Hill
    p.   cm.
Includes bibliographical references.
ISBN 1-59098-660-1 (alk. paper)
1. Libraries—Ohio—History. 2. Public Libraries—Ohio—Histories
I. Hill, Melinda F., 1978– II. Title.
   Z732.O5B47 2003
   027.0771—dc22   2003018711

∞ The paper used in this publication meets the minimum requirements of the American National Standard for Information Services—Permanence of Paper for Printed Library Materials, ANSI Z39.48-1992.

*Dedicated to the next two hundred years of Ohio libraries—
May Ohio's libraries continue to change and improve
the lives of all of our state's residents.*

Table of Contents

Foreword, *Amos J. Loveday* 1

CHAPTER 1
Ohio Public Libraries Serving the Local Communities,
  Stephen Hedges and Alan Hall 7

CHAPTER 2
The Buildings of Ohio's Public Libraries, *H. Baird Tenney*
  and Rachel Wayne Nelson 23
  The Sandusky Library: A Case Study, *Barbara Bishop* 34
  An Early Library Building: A Case Study, *H. Baird Tenney*
    and Rachel Wayne Nelson 36
  Enter the ADA: A Case Study, *H. Baird Tenney*
    and Rachel Wayne Nelson 37
  Where's That Card Catalog? A Case Study,
    H. Baird Tenney and Rachel Wayne Nelson 38

CHAPTER 3
Clear Heads, Strong Hands, and Great Hearts: The Staff
  of Ohio's Libraries, *Harriet Clem and Margaret Albright* 39
  Burton Stevenson: A Case Study, *Jennifer Thompson* 51

CHAPTER 4
Serving Every Citizen: Ohio's Library Patrons,
  Outreach Services, and Friends Groups, *Melinda F. Hill* 53

CHAPTER 5
Library Trustees, *David C. Miller* 65

CHAPTER 6
Intellectual Freedom, *Jeff French and Cindy Lombardo* 77
  Defending the Right to Information: A Case Study, *Jeff French* ...90

CHAPTER 7
The Future of Ohio's Libraries, *Steve Wood* 91

CHAPTER 8
Cornerstones and Landmarks in Ohio Library History,
   Jay Ladd 97

CHAPTER 9
Model Library Histories 131

Bibliography 135

Author Biographies 141

Best in the Nation

Foreword

IN JUNE 1997, AFTER VISITING OHIO, John Berry, Editor-in-Chief of the *Library Journal*, wrote, "if you want to watch academic and public librarians at work creating the future ... be sure to take a look at Ohio." Berry's comments came at a particularly heady time, just as the Ohio library community was beginning to confront the challenges of the electronic revolution. Berry certainly had the challenges of the late 1990s in mind when he penned his comments. But, as authors of this book show, Berry's comment could have been made on almost any day of any month of any year during the twentieth century. Indeed, Ohio librarians have been hard at work creating the future since the days when canal boats and Conestoga wagons were cutting edge technology. This book is about their cumulative efforts, which over generations have produced a remarkable group of institutions that are simply the best of their kind in the nation.

The following pages tell the story of how the best came to be, not as a chronological narrative, but from the perspective of the groups that shaped individual libraries and the system as a whole. While there have been differences of opinion within the community over the years, these groups have shared several fundamental beliefs that provided the foundation for a long and fruitful relationship between libraries and the people of Ohio.

To a remarkable extent, those associated with Ohio libraries have had a clear understanding that their business was, and is, the promotion of literacy, both as traditionally defined, and in new forms as the definition has changed over time. When literacy was understood as *reading skills*, libraries promoted reading; but when literacy came to encompass understanding the Internet, Ohio librarians took on the task of narrowing the digital divide.

Many members of the Ohio library community also share a long and deeply held understanding that their primary mission is to provide information, rather than to warehouse books or, in more recent times, to be a portal to the Internet. Put differently, Ohio libraries have been remarkably successful at keeping their mission and their tools in proper perspective, a quality that has allowed them to embrace new information media as a logical step rather than as a new departure. Informed by patron interests, libraries comfortably made space on their shelves for new communications technologies ranging from LP records to videotapes and the Internet.

The timely acceptance of the Internet in particular demonstrates that Ohio libraries have a keen sense of whom they serve. When they discovered that their patrons were *logging on*, they moved quickly to serve those already cruising the "information superhighway" and to assist others who were sizing up, in some cases warily, its potential. This was not atypical behavior.

Libraries have been first and foremost local institutions that serve the communities in which they are located. Indeed, in Ohio *local* and *library* appear side-by-side so often that it is difficult to speak or write of libraries without inserting the adjective. Because Ohio libraries are *of the communities* they serve, they have come to know, listen to, and trust their users in ways few other institutions comprehend.

Few institutions have sought to serve such a broad demographic audience and none have gone to greater lengths to make their services as accessible. Ohio libraries' insistence on *free* access welcomes all people, no matter their economic station, while a commitment to *life-long learning*—a new phrase to be sure—invites citizens from the kindergarten or senior citizen center to *belly up* to the circulation desk to place their order.

This *service to all citizens* approach has been the foundation for Ohio libraries' success at garnering financial, as well as moral, support. Most communities, for example, have had more faith in their librarians' professional judgment—guided by local boards' sensitivity to community standards—rather than the censor's rule book, as guidance for the patron's journey through the world of words, images, and thoughts.

While Ohio libraries have concentrated their energies on the local community in matters of service, they have cast far afield for models of how that service should be delivered. From the days when the citizens of Amesville collected animal pelts to pay for the storied Coonskin Library, to the recent past when the library community set out to equalize funding for the state's libraries, Ohio librarians and trustees have been innovators in the financing of library services. Here, as in matters of mission, a belief that libraries serve—and must ultimately be accountable to—local citizens has been a guiding principle.

Across the state and over the years, Ohio citizens have repeatedly approved of their libraries commitment to the community, certainty of mission, and innovative approaches. Voters in community after community have supported libraries at the ballot box; citizens in every corner of the state have demonstrated their faith in librarians' professional judgment; and patrons in villages and cities of every size have volunteered to serve on boards or with Friends groups.

Almost everyone who has had the opportunity to talk about Ohio libraries in settings beyond the state's borders has encountered disbelief, amazement, and even envy from audiences that hear of the support our system receives. Alan Hall, one of the authors of the historical overview that appears in this book, is fond of recounting a conversation with out-of-state librarians who wanted to know how they could make their libraries as good as Ohio libraries. His response, "change history," hints at a major theme of *Best in the Nation*. Ohio libraries did not just happen. They are the handiwork—to call again upon John Berry's observation—of people who worked to create the future. So, while *Best in the Nation* is a history of how the system came to be, the reader should be advised that it is the history of a community that held the present and the future in a tighter embrace than the past.

In the final analysis then, this history of Ohio's libraries not only seeks to explain how the best library system in the nation came to be, but if I read the authors correctly, how they want to encourage an appreciation of the forward-looking professionals, volunteers, and community leaders who built a truly impressive edifice.

—AMOS J. LOVEDAY, Ph.D.
Historian, former library trustee, author, and lover of libraries

Acknowledgements

The production of this book involved the work of many people besides the authors listed. To start at the beginning, Fran Haley first conceived the notion of a book about the history of Ohio's public libraries as part of the Ohio Library Council's celebration of the Ohio Bicentennial, and then ably shepherded the project through its formative years, with assistance from Meribah Mansfield and Mary Jane Santos. Scores of people (too many to name) donated copies of their local library histories. Dr. David Kyvig provided the benefit of his experience as an editor and writer of local histories and contributed valuable advice on making this book more than just a list of names and dates. Lynda Murray contributed funding information and advice. Several people, most notably John Philip, shared gems of information and interesting photographs they had found. David Wiesenberg went beyond the normal duties of a publisher and contributed valuable advice on turning the manuscripts into a real book. And finally, Stephen Hedges, though one of the authors, also served as the "straw boss" of this project, coordinating communications and efforts among all the contributors.

Ohio Public Libraries Serving the Local Communities
STEPHEN HEDGES and ALAN HALL

OHIO HAS SUCCESSFULLY DEVELOPED the best public library network in the nation. Tracing the history of Ohio's public libraries is valuable because many important lessons can be learned from Ohio's success story. But any such history is even more valuable in light of the fact that the history of Ohio's public libraries is intertwined with the history of Ohio and the nation. Public libraries do not spring up from nothing; they are rooted in the communities that create and support them. Public libraries are tightly woven into the fabric of the communities which house them, and that fabric is and always has been shaped and colored by the same forces that have influenced the development of American society in general. Thus this chapter not only lists some of the names and dates that are important in Ohio library history, but also makes mention of the larger social trends and events in American and Ohio history that have affected the relationships between libraries and the people they serve. The authors would refer readers looking for a more "facts-based" history of Ohio libraries to the excellent "Cornerstones and Landmarks in Ohio Library History" by the late Jay Ladd, an important piece of research that is reproduced elsewhere in this volume. Rather than replicating Ladd's work, the following history seeks to interpret the facts of Ohio library history and place them in a larger context.

Humble Beginnings

Amos Dunham came to the Ohio country in 1802 as a young man. He was without property, a trade, or profession. His first home consisted of a camp of poles, constructed on sixty acres of land purchased on credit. A loaf of bread, a piece of pickled pork, potatoes, and a borrowed frying pan completed his household on the Ohio frontier.

A log house followed, with a handmade bedstead. Dunham was ten miles from Ohio's first settlement at Marietta and six miles from Ohio's second settlement of Belle Prairie, now called Belpre. Such were the hardships of the early settlers arriving from New England and Virginia to claim their piece of the new lands.

Amos Dunham told Ohio historian Henry Howe in 1847 that the "long winter evenings were rather tedious, and in order to make them pass more smoothly, by great exertion, I purchased a share in the Belpre Library.

"[While this] promised myself much entertainment, another obstacle presented itself—I had no candles. However, the woods afforded plenty of pine knots—with these I made torches by which I could read." Thus, with the problem of lighting solved, one of Ohio's first library patrons began reading "until 12 or 1 o'clock" in the morning, according to Dunham (Howe, 349–350).

Amos Dunham was also one of the first library trustees in Ohio. As a loyal patron of the subscription library of which he was a member, Dunham served as a trustee, and his wife noted that her husband "could always find time to attend the meetings of the Belpre Library regardless of the pressure of other work."

The first settlers of Ohio likely carried precious few books with them across the Allegheny Mountains. Lists of the collections of the early pioneers can be found in the archives of the Marietta College Library, and demonstrate that books of practical skills were the likely books carefully packed for the trip. Surveying, agriculture, and religion were common subjects for the books. Concerns of intellectual growth were tempered by the reality of life on the Ohio frontier.

Often the early libraries started as the collection of a "great man" of the day. One such man was Colonel Israel Putnam, the eldest son of

Revolutionary War General Israel Putnam. The younger Putnam came to Marietta in the winter of 1788–89 and chose a tract of land near Belpre. He returned to his native Connecticut to complete business affairs, and during that time his father died. It was 1795 before Colonel Putnam returned to Belpre, bringing seeds for planting. He also brought back other seeds—books. His share of the Putnam Family Library made the trek to the Ohio country.

The books had been gathered by his father, and formed a collection which the Colonel shared with his neighbors, both far and near. The number of books is unknown, but shares were sold in the Putnam Family Library and documented in 1796 as an entry in the Washington County Probate Court Records: "Received of Jonathan Stone, by the hand of Benjamin Mills, ten dollars, for his share in the Putnam Family Library." Stone's share was documented again in 1801 as part of the inventory for his estate.

Ten dollars was a considerable sum of money for the day, acknowledging the importance of a library share to the settlers on the Ohio frontier. Sometime after 1796, the name changed to Belpre Farmer's Library. Isaac Pierce became the librarian and keeper of the books that had now passed out of the Putnam family. According to tradition, the Belpre Farmer's Library resided in a wicker basket under the librarian's bed. The library continued for many years, dissolved by mutual consent in 1815, with the books distributed to members. Only six volumes remain today and those relate to agriculture, history, and theology.

The Belpre Farmer's Library established the beginning of the history of Ohio libraries, beginning just before the dawn of the nineteenth century. As the century progressed, it became clear that a library was a source of pride for any community that established one. Several communities debated which library was the "first" in the state. That debate was addressed in the 1880s by the Honorable John Eaton, United States Commissioner of Education. He accepted the decision of a group of Ohio literary scholars who felt that the 1796 record of the sale of shares in the Putnam Family Library documented that it was then a circulating library and establishes it as Ohio's first library. The fact that the issue reached this level of discussion demonstrates the importance that communities place in their library. Today, the Belpre Branch of the

Washington County Public Library is the direct descendant of the Farmer's Library and continues the tradition of library service to that community.

Ohio's second library is documented in a newspaper story from the *Western Spy and Hamilton Gazette* of February 15, 1802:

> At a meeting held on Saturday evening, the 13th instant, at Mr. Yeatman's tavern, for the purpose of promoting the establishment of a public library in the town of Cincinnati, Messrs. Jacob Burnet, Martin Baum, and Lewis Kerr were appointed [as] a committee to open a subscription for carrying the above project into effect.

The committee submitted a subscription form and raised $340, with Lewis Kerr chosen as librarian. The roots of the Cincinnati Library were planted.

Commonly (but erroneously) considered the first library in Ohio, the "Coonskin Library" in Amesville was officially established on February 2, 1804, in the home of Silvanus Ames. The library had begun to form a year earlier when a quantity of furs were collected and sent to New York in the care of Samuel Brown. The "coonskins" were sold for $73.50, from which the initial collection of the library was purchased. The library was chartered by legislative act in 1810 as the "Western Library Association," adopting the more common name of Coonskin Library due to the unusual nature of the original funding source. Unlike many of the early subscription libraries, this library enjoyed a healthy fifty-seven-year span of library service to its community.

There were many connections of families between the settlements at Belpre and Amesville. The Belpre Library may have influenced the establishment of the Coonskin Library. It was reported that three graduates of Harvard College lived in the community, encouraging the literary establishment of a circulating library on the Ohio frontier. Today, a small museum in Amesville celebrates this library and its colorful history, and many of the earliest materials of the library are preserved by the Ohio Historical Society in Columbus.

The establishment of the Social Library of Dayton in 1805 marked the beginning of the establishment and incorporation of libraries through an act of the new State legislature. Prior to laws governing the establishment of libraries, the sponsoring institution had to incorporate with the Ohio Secretary of State's office with approval of the legislature. This was followed by the Granville Alexandrian Society Library as the second incorporated library in Ohio. The first library organized in the Western Reserve portion of Ohio was at Poland, Ohio, in 1810, and the following year saw the establishment of Cleveland's first Library Association.

Prior to 1817, a special law was passed each time a subscription library was incorporated. Records show twenty such libraries in Ohio, with another seventeen in the planning stage, when the legislature passed an overall law covering the incorporation of schools and library companies. While this law provided for the incorporation of public libraries, it made no provisions for their support.

This same year saw the establishment of the State Library of Ohio to serve state government officials. Governor Thomas Worthington purchased 509 books while in Philadelphia, books that covered not only great literature, but biographies, travel, law, Bibles, and the same types of "practical" books on agriculture and manual trades that were common in the public libraries of the state. These books were the beginning of the State Library.

One hundred twenty new libraries were formed from 1824 to 1840. Early Ohio historian Caleb Atwater stated that "by 1838 most towns had reading rooms and that libraries were increasing in numbers as well as size" (Atwater, 348). New formats of libraries were also beginning to form in Ohio. These replaced or supplemented subscription libraries in purpose and function. Commercial libraries rented books from stores in the towns. Reading rooms opened under various sponsorships to stock newspapers and periodicals. The Lyceum Movement pursued higher learning through lectures, discussions, and research and had as one of its goals to "call into use neglected libraries and giving occasion for establishing new ones." Many times the Lyceum and the local library occupied the same building in a community.

The Lyceum Movement was an outgrowth of a larger trend toward emphasis on education, particularly education for the "common man," as opposed to the "gentleman." It arose in the climate of industrial growth and Jacksonian democracy that began to empower many of the "blue collar" workers in the United States, and was an intentional effort to break down the stratification of American society, which at this point was strongly divided by race, ethnicity, and wealth. Public schools and public libraries were important focal points of the movement.

In many areas, local academies and schools allowed the public to use their library facilities. Sometimes private individuals shared their books with the public, as happened in the 1830s, when Steubenville native Edwin M. Stanton, later Lincoln's Secretary of War, opened his house and his book collection for public use for a small fee. The 1850 census showed sixty-five public libraries in Ohio, with a total collection of 65,703 volumes. The same statistics also showed that 200 Ohio communities had made futile attempts to maintain a library.

A major landmark in the history of public libraries in Ohio came in the form of the School Act of 1853, which marked an end to many subscription libraries and lyceums. This act provided for a state school tax, free education for all youth, and a fund of one-tenth of a mill on all taxable property for the purpose of furnishing school libraries. The property tax for library funding was abolished in 1860, as the Civil War began to claim more government resources, but the School Act is often considered to be the beginning of the free public library movement in Ohio. Up to this point, in fact, only the libraries in Cincinnati and Dayton were strictly public libraries. This act had a haphazard effect, with libraries closing and reopening over the next thirty years; it was difficult to develop a library collection without a consistent base of funds. Yet, during the seven years of tax funding, 400,000 books were distributed by the state commissioner of common schools to school libraries.

A Redefined America

The Civil War completely redefined American society, changing the way Americans treated each other and shifting the focus of society toward urban areas. These changes would eventually have a profound effect on the development of public libraries in Ohio. The years following the war have been called "The Age of Exploitation," as industrialists who had built their businesses by supplying the needs of the armies scrambled for land, power, and wealth. The concept of "Social Darwinism" became widely published and was used to justify the destruction of the Plains Indians and prejudice against blacks and immigrants. American society was still deeply stratified, and interest in providing for the edification of the general public waned.

An 1869 Ohio law allowed municipalities to open and maintain libraries and reading rooms for the public. This legislation actually recognized four types of libraries—municipal, township, school district, or county, depending on the taxing authority used to support the library. Numerous Ohio cities took advantage of this law, with large numbers of new public libraries established from former libraries. The establishment of the American Library Association in 1876, and later the Ohio Library Association in 1895, stimulated library service to the state with structured assistance and research about libraries.

Many new developments in American society in the last quarter of the nineteenth century occurred in the growing urban areas. Services such as transport systems and public utilities were initiated in many cities during this time period. Likewise, urban libraries pioneered new services during these years.

In 1871, Cincinnati opened the library on Sundays, and then opened the first branch library in Ohio at Cumminsville in 1879. Electra Doren, later one of the founders of the Ohio Library Association, introduced dictionary card cataloging at the Dayton Public Library in 1880. Under the leadership of William Howard Brett, later the first president of the Ohio Library Association, Cleveland opened a separate children's room in the main library in 1898. In 1901, Cincinnati Public Library began offering story hours for children on Saturday mornings.

The establishment of the Ohio Library Association was at least partially motivated by a renewed interest in free public libraries that spread from the cities of the northeastern United States to the Midwest at the close of the century. Once again, as with the Lyceum Movement, this push for more libraries had its genesis in widespread efforts by progressive elements of society to bridge the gap between the rich and the poor. During the five years from 1891 to 1896, twenty-nine new libraries and library branches were opened in Ohio, making a total of 202, and matching the growth rate for libraries nationwide. Ohio libraries held a combined total of more than 1.5 million books.

In 1896, major changes in the State Library of Ohio redefined its purpose. While the original State Library had limited its circulation to state officials, and was headed by a librarian appointed either by the General Assembly or by the governor, a law was now enacted to place the State Library under a commission appointed by the governor. This commission was given the authority to adopt rules for management and to choose the State Librarian. They chose Charles Galbreath, who wrote in his *History of Ohio* in 1925:

> Promptly after the enactment of this law, rules were adopted extending the service of the library to citizens of the state, and providing for the loan of books not only to individuals but through the traveling library system to communities. (Galbreath, I:513)

Galbreath established these traveling libraries, and soon Sunday schools, women's clubs, Grange halls, and clubs of all descriptions received collections of books. This had the effect of creating an interest in the establishment of new local libraries. Ten years later, in 1906, the Office of Library Organizer was formed at the State Library to provide professional assistance to local communities in establishing a library.

County library legislation enabling tax-supported county libraries was passed in 1898, and libraries serving the whole county were formed in Van Wert and Hamilton Counties. By the turn of the century, three-fourths of Ohio counties contained library service of some type. In 1900, there were 146 public libraries in Ohio, 162 public school libraries, and forty-seven special libraries. The U.S. Bureau of Education reported that 266 of these libraries contained more than 1,000 volumes, and statewide there were more than two million books in libraries. Ohio's libraries had made mighty strides in their first century.

The Funding Question

With the traveling libraries exciting a demand for more public libraries in Ohio, the question that now arose was how to pay for them. Government funding was certainly not the answer. The federal government in particular had been very ineffective and even corrupt in the last years of the nineteenth century, and was just embarking on the reforms of the "Progressive Era" as the century turned. Municipal governments were more responsive to the needs of the people in some communities, most notably in Toledo and Cleveland, but this was not the case in every city. Where was the funding for new libraries to come from?

The answer to the question came in the form of philanthropy, specifically donations from the wealthy. In fact, the county library legislation of 1898 had been made necessary by the gift of a building for the purpose of creating the Brumback Library, the first county library in the world. But the most important donations came from the steel magnate, Andrew Carnegie, whose contributions are chronicled at length in the following chapter on library buildings.

In Ohio, the state government was preparing the ground during the early years of the twentieth century for eventually shouldering most of the burden of funding public libraries. Various pieces of legislation passed by the General Assembly between 1910 and 1930 experimented with tax support of public libraries, usually through real estate taxes, which could be levied by schools for the purpose of supporting a library open to the public.

The most important of these laws, passed in 1921, allowed school districts to levy a library tax on real estate that went beyond the 1% limitation on property taxes that had been established by the Smith One Percent Act in 1911. As a result, many municipal libraries were turned over to school boards, since the schools were now permitted to ask taxpayers for more library support than the city could. When the legislation passed in 1921, there were thirty-three school district libraries in Ohio; six years later, there were 105. In 1929, however, on the eve of the Great Depression, an Ohio constitutional amendment limited the total of all real estate taxes to ten mills, effectively eliminating real estate taxes as the major source of revenue for public libraries.

This is a critical juncture in the history of Ohio's public libraries, and the events of the years around 1930 made it possible for Ohio's public libraries to begin their long climb to "best in the nation." At this point, the state government could have abandoned the responsibility for funding public libraries to municipalities, school districts, other local government agencies, or philanthropy, with only limited assistance from state funds. In many states, this is exactly the way public libraries are still funded. But such a funding system would not have supplied the stable foundation that made steady advancement of public library service possible.

Fortunately, the General Assembly did not abandon the public libraries. In 1931, State Senator Robert Taft fathered the Ohio County Intangible Tax Law, which was approved by the Ohio Supreme Court in 1933. This had several long-term effects on public libraries. First, it provided a stable funding system, which could be augmented by local levies that continued to support libraries for over fifty years. It also had the effect of encouraging public library service to all the citizens of Ohio, since it only provided funds to libraries which made themselves freely available to all residents of the county in which they were located. Finally, it established a tradition of strong state support of public libraries, allowing libraries to exist in poor areas where local tax levies could not have supported a public library. It ensured, in effect, that at least basic library service was available to every citizen of the state.

Rapid Library Expansion

Under the leadership of State Librarian Paul A.T. Noon, consultants from the State Library fanned out across Ohio in the 1930s assisting public libraries with their plans to expand library services to the entire county. Many libraries became "County Extension Centers" as a result and nearly every part of the state had library service through main libraries, branch libraries, or bookmobile services.

In 1945, the legislature appointed the Ohio Library Survey Commission to study the now rapidly expanding base of public libraries. As a result of the study, the legislature ended the establishment of any more new public libraries effective September 4, 1947. Only countywide libraries could be established after that date, or branches of existing libraries. The number of public library districts in Ohio declined from 280 in 1947 to 250 in 1970. This was a very positive move, taking library establishment from a haphazard endeavor to a systematic one, ensuring enough funding for established libraries.

Cooperation between libraries became a priority for larger public and academic libraries in Ohio in the mid-1930s. In 1936, the publication of the "Regional List of Serials in the College and University Libraries in Ohio" also contained a "Code of Practice for Interlibrary Loans," signaling a growing interest in sharing resources between libraries. The following year, the State Library of Ohio began work on a Union Catalog of the holdings of the largest public libraries, and Ohio became the first state in the nation to have such a centralized library catalog. A more direct example of resource sharing came in 1948, when the Cleveland Public Library inaugurated an educational film circuit that distributed 16MM films to ten libraries in the area around Cleveland. Note that this service is also evidence that libraries were now collecting information in formats other than books.

By this time, the intangibles tax funding of public libraries was in need of some attention. The intangibles tax revenues received within each county were distributed by the county budget commission on the basis of "need." Just how this need was defined and measured became a point of contention. Often the decision was based on a tradition established over time of giving each library a predetermined percentage, rather than making an annual judgment as to the current needs of each library. But some counties developed funding formulas based on the population each library served and the previous year's circulation statistics. Thus the stage was often set for discord among the libraries serving a county.

One other problem with the intangibles tax was the fact that some counties collected very little revenue from this source, while other counties fared well. Since the tax revenue depended on the number of county residents who owned investments, some libraries, particularly in rural areas, received very little funding. So while public libraries in Ohio did have a well-established source of state funds, the funding system itself was not equitable.

The problems faced by rural libraries were receiving national attention at about this time. In 1956, the federal government passed the Library Services Act (LSA), which established grants to states for the purpose of improving rural library services. The State Library of Ohio immediately used these funds to set up rural library service centers and bookmobile programs.

Rural and small libraries also began to band together to share whatever resources they had. The Southwestern Ohio Rural Libraries Council (SWORL) was founded in 1962 and received LSA Title I funds in 1968. In southeastern Ohio, the Ohio Valley Area Libraries (OVAL) was formed in 1969 and officially chartered as Ohio's first Area Library Service Organization (ALSO) in 1973. In 1970, the State Library used LSA funds to assist multi-library cooperatives. In short order, this led to the development of the Miami Valley Library Organization (MILO) [now MVL] and the Southeastern Ohio Library Organization (SOLO) in 1970, the Mideastern Ohio Library Organization (MOLO) and the Central Ohio Interlibrary Network (COIN) in 1971, the Northeastern Ohio Library Association (NOLA) in 1972, and the Northwestern Library District (NORWELD) in 1973. As with SWORL and OVAL, the cooperatives shared resources and provided opportunities for small and rural libraries to make group purchases at a discount. They would later provide training and technology assistance to member libraries.

By the beginning of the 1980s, Ohio libraries were working in an environment of relatively stable state funding and increasing opportunities for cooperation. New developments were soon to take both funding and cooperation to new levels. In the early 1980s, computerized library circulation and catalog systems began to be more common. This led to a new type of cooperation between libraries: the shared catalog and automation system. In 1981, the State Library of Ohio and the Ohio State University agreed to share a computer catalog. The following year, the Cleveland Heights-University Heights Library asked to join the

Cleveland Public Library's computerized system, thus starting the Clevnet computer network. As of the end of 2002, Clevnet served thirty-one library systems in nine northern Ohio counties.

In 1981, a meeting was held at the St. Clairsville Public Library announcing that the State Library planned to automate the SEO Library Center. The SEO Center had been established as the Southeastern Ohio Regional Library Center in 1961, using funds from the federal Library Services Act. Like the other five centers in Ohio, SEO was opened as a branch of the State Library of Ohio to service rural areas of the state with reference service, interlibrary loan, and bookmobile service under contract to local libraries.

The 1981 meeting in St. Clairsville notified area libraries of the State Library's plans to automate the SEO Center, and sought to gauge how much interest libraries in the SEO service area had in joining the project. These were the early days of shared library automation, and the technology was untested to link libraries over a fourteen-county area. Four libraries became charter members of the SEO Automation System, including the Public Library of Steubenville and Jefferson County, Puskarich Public Library of Cadiz, St. Clairsville Public Library, and the Monroe County District Library in Woodsfield. The Barnesville-Hutton Memorial Library joined shortly after the system became operational.

By 1993, seven more SEO area libraries had joined the system. With the availability of Internet connections and the progression of communication technology, SEO has now grown to include libraries all across Ohio. One hundred fifty libraries in sixty-five library systems are part of SEO today. They share 5.2 million items through statewide five-day-per-week delivery service, with requests placed online into the system by users.

The 1980s brought a major change to state funding. For years, the inequity of the intangibles tax base across the state had resulted in inequitable funding of public libraries. In 1982, the opportunity arose to correct this: the state decided to incorporate the intangibles tax into the personal income tax. In order to replace the intangibles tax funds that went to public libraries (and a few other local government entities), it was determined that 6.3% of personal income tax receipts would need to be set aside into a special fund, called the Library and Local Government Support Fund (LLGSF).

Having established the fund, the question now became one of how to distribute the money to libraries without replicating the inequities of the intangibles tax. During the course of 1983, a committee consisting of legislators, librarians, educators, and financial experts worked out the details of what came to be known as the "Equalization Formula." The goal of this formula was ideally to reach a point where funds distributed to public library systems were approximately equal when calculated per person living in the library's service area. For various reasons, the Equalization Formula has yet to achieve truly equal per capita funding, though most of the inequalities of state funding for public libraries have been alleviated. Ohio's public libraries now enjoy relatively stable and equal state funding, something that has not yet been achieved elsewhere in the nation.

Life after Stable Funding

With public libraries now receiving funds from the LLGSF, two things began to happen. First, individual libraries began to construct new buildings and implement expanded services, a change most noticeable in the small and rural libraries that may not have received many funds from the intangibles tax. Second, the 250 public library systems in Ohio embarked on some aggressive initiatives to share resources to an extent not seen before.

Much of the resource sharing begun after the advent of the LLGSF was made possible by technology and inspired by OhioLink, a statewide network of academic libraries that began operating in 1992. OhioLink used Internet connections to tie the academic libraries together, then mandated that all of these libraries would use the same integrated library automation system, using funds supplied by the state to pay for the change from their previous automation systems. This allowed the users of these libraries to search the catalogs of all the libraries and request that the items be sent from remote libraries to their local library. In effect, OhioLink turned the academic libraries into one huge, distributed library that stretched across the state.

OhioLink libraries also shared access to online databases, benefiting from discounts received by banding together to buy rights to these databases one time and then sharing them across the network.

Public libraries now began two initiatives aimed at emulating the level of resource sharing achieved by OhioLink, but without compromising the local autonomy that public libraries enjoyed. This tradition of autonomy dictated that any resource sharing would have to allow local library boards to continue to select the automation system they felt best fit their needs. In fact, by the time all public libraries had library automation systems installed, there were almost twenty different systems in use across the state, each using slightly different data formats, user interfaces, and protocols. This made any resource-sharing project vastly more complex than it had been for OhioLink libraries.

The first task was to connect all of Ohio's public library systems to the Internet, and then use these connections to feed online information and data to the libraries, and to allow library users free access to information available on the World Wide Web. Planning for the Ohio Public Library Information Network (OPLIN) was completed by the end of 1994, and the network became operational in June, 1996. The overriding rationale for OPLIN was to ensure that all Ohio citizens had equal access to information. OPLIN currently provides the residents of Ohio fast, free Internet access through their local public libraries, as well as the use of high-quality research databases not freely available on the World Wide Web.

The second task was to provide a mechanism for searching library catalogs and shipping items quickly from library to library. Planning for this system, which came to be called MORE ("Moving Ohio Resources Everywhere"), began only a few years after OPLIN became fully operational, and implementation of the system began in 2002. The MORE system is intended to be a statewide circulation system, initially involving the state's public and school libraries, but with the potential to include academic and special libraries. The goal of MORE is to allow any library user to request an item from any Ohio library and check it out from the user's home library. The system includes a statewide delivery network and software that handles catalog searches between different types of automation systems.

Best in the Nation

In the twentieth century, then, Ohio's public libraries expanded their service to include all of the citizens of Ohio, with a multitude of library buildings covering the entire state. In the waning years of the century, they used strong government support and advanced technology to provide Ohioans with unprecedented access to materials and information located outside their local library buildings. As a result, the people of Ohio enjoy a public library system that many have judged to be the best in the nation, and can look forward to even better library service in the future.

> ### *And Ladies ...*
>
> Ohio's leadership in the nation became apparent with the 1942 publication of the book *County Library Primer* by State Library Consultant Mildred W. Sandoe and her colleague Helen Santmyer, better known today for the later publication of her novel ... *And Ladies of the Club.*

The Buildings of Ohio's Public Libraries
H. Baird Tenney and Rachel Wayne Nelson

According to State Librarian Michael Lucas, there are 711 public library buildings in Ohio: one main building for each of the state's 250 systems and 461 branches. These buildings are an extremely diverse lot, ranging from grand to humble and from contemporary to truly historic. Though none are as grand as the Great Library that once stood in Alexandria, each has a look and a history worth preserving.

We are not prepared to put a capital valuation on all public library buildings now in use. It would be an enormous sum made more impressive by the fact that it represents investment largely of local source funds supplemented by the government. Moreover, in virtually every case, the initiative for local library building projects comes from the local community and is carried out by the library management, urged on in many cases by individuals desiring to make a memorial gift. Andrew Carnegie is one of many who have provided generously for the building of Ohio's libraries.

Carnegie Grants Spread Libraries Far and Wide

Andrew Carnegie (1835–1919), a co-founder of the modern American steel industry, was also a "co-founder" of Ohio public libraries or, more specifically, Ohio's library buildings. From his personal resources he financed the construction of 111 library buildings in Ohio during the early twentieth century. There were seventy-eight separate grants in this truly revolutionary period.

Ohio was fifth among the states in Carnegie grants, and the Midwest (Ohio to the Dakotas) was by far the leader, with 53% of total grants. Most of the Carnegie buildings in Ohio and elsewhere are still in use as libraries, though all have been modified to bring them in line with modern requirements.

Carnegie grants were carefully calculated to cover the cost of design and construction only. Not the site. Not the collection of books. In addition, the municipality had to pass legislation providing public funds for library operation. Funds were normally disbursed in incremental checks. The ultimate source of funds was the impressive profitability of Mr. Carnegie's steel and other enterprises. He was an investor and manager of extraordinary skill.

By chance, a book describing the Carnegie phenomenon in Ohio has just been published by Mary Ellen Armentrout, director of the Herrick Memorial Library in Wellington. The book is a must-read for all who are interested in Ohio libraries and is a major source for this chapter on library buildings. Theodore Jones' *Carnegie Libraries Across America* covers Carnegie libraries nationally.

The Armentrout book represents four years of research in visiting and photographing every Carnegie site in the state. In addition to the author's photos, a number of historic views are included, coming from the Ohio Historical Society and other sources. Each Carnegie grant is described and illustrated, showing current views of those buildings that continue as libraries and a few buildings that have been cleverly converted to other uses.

More than half of the Carnegie buildings are still used as libraries. Considering that the youngest buildings are over eighty years old, this is a remarkable record of survival. Many newer public buildings have long since disappeared, sometimes thankfully. But the Carnegie buildings were, for the most part, well designed and certainly were well received by the towns where they were built. All the survivors have been remodeled a time or more and added to, frequently in a way that harmonizes with the original design. Not so fortunate were the ten, but only ten, Carnegie buildings that have been demolished. Some, no doubt, deserved their fate, but other sturdy Carnegie buildings have withstood fire, flood, neglect, and excessive "modernization."

As the last of the Carnegie buildings was completed in 1919 or 1920, there were about 3500 public library buildings in the U.S.—half of them built with Carnegie funds. Perhaps dozens or even hundreds more were financed by local people who chose to honor Carnegie by imitation.

The Carnegie Way

The sequence of steps by which a Carnegie building came to be seem simple today. There was in the Carnegie method no place for conflicting levels of review and approval as may be found today. Here is how Carnegie did it:

1. No publicity.

The first Carnegie grants in Ohio were in towns with some tie to the steel industry (Sandusky, 1901; East Liverpool, 1902; and Steubenville, 1902). Steel connections were certainly not required, and interested grantees seemed to hear about the program from neighboring towns.

2. Start with a letter request.

In the case of Amherst, a Wm. H. Schibley of the library board wrote to Mr. Carnegie in 1903 about the "... necessity and benefits for a library in our town and ask your assistance and advice in this manner." A few months later the board followed up with details, adding "We will all try hard with your aid to have something good and your money will not be misplaced." A promise of $10,000 was received a few weeks later and the project was soon underway. Judith Dworkin, director at Amherst, included these notes from the past in "Keeping our pledge to Mr. Carnegie," an article about the building's recent renovation (*Ohio Libraries*, Winter 2002).

3. Basic terms.

Grants were generally written on the basis of $2.00 per person by the latest census. Further, the sponsors had to provide a site in a good location and debt-free. Moreover, the town government had to provide continuing annual support of at least 10% of the construction grant. Legislation was required. Promises were not enough.

4. Bargaining—Occasionally.

The donor's interests were represented by James Bertram (1872–1934), a private secretary to Mr. Carnegie and later secretary to the Carnegie Corporation. He was the law on the nature of library grants and ran things in a very businesslike way. For example, the formula called for Napoleon, Ohio, to get $10,000, but when bids were opened, the town asked for another $2,500 to cover possible overruns. Nineteen letters passed back and forth between parties but Mr. Bertram held firm at $10,000. New, lower bids were requested and received and the new building was dedicated in mid-1913. Note that bargaining was sometimes successful. In 1904, Bellevue was offered $10,000, later asked for another $2,600, and got it.

5. Design Matters.

Early in the Carnegie program there were few architects and fewer boards with experience in designing small-town libraries. Bertram found great vexation and waste in this and in 1911 (subsequently revised) issued his manifesto on design: TO OBTAIN FOR THE MONEY THE UTMOST AMOUNT OF EFFECTIV ACCOMODATION, CONSISTENT WITH GOOD TAST IN BILDING (Note that Bertram and Carnegie believed in simplified spelling). With this very brief document, including some sample floor plans, a higher degree of rationality soon prevailed. Individual architects picked by the community were the ones who solved many problems and provided the classic "come hither" look at the front door of so many Carnegie buildings. Bertram reviewed plans, with great help from Cleveland librarian William Howard Brett, but never, in spite of many requests, sent out a ready-made set of plans.

6. Final Steps.

Once the terms and conditions of the grant were agreed to, the funds were paid out in three equal installments: at groundbreaking, when the foundation was finished, and upon completion of the project.

Why Did He Do It?

Explanations for the great support Andrew Carnegie provided for public library construction generally center on his experiences as a young lad newly arrived from Scotland. Unable to attend school because he was the family breadwinner, he sought and was granted permission to borrow books from the private library of Colonel James Anderson of what is now Pittsburgh. This is undoubtedly a strong motivation, but there were other personal and circumstantial influences as well. Here are a few possibilities:

1. His belief that reading is fundamental for individual and community progress.

Carnegie believed this, and such statements have echoed down through the ages. Archibald MacLeish at the Carnegie Institute in 1939 said "[libraries] are the only institutions in American life capable of opening to the citizens of the Republic knowledge of the wealth and richness of the culture. ..." Ohio's own former State Librarian and now New York State Librarian Emeritus, Joseph F. Shubert, said in a speech in Albany in January 2002, "Our libraries are rooted in the aspirations of a free society."

2. Profitability of Carnegie enterprises.

The Carnegie library program was, of course, financed through the profitability of the properties he controlled, mostly in the iron and steel industry. Carnegie saw the advantages of large-scale industry and promoted advances in cost accounting so as to better understand ways to improve profitability. Moreover, profits and personal income remained largely untaxed until 1911.

3. Capital for the public sector.

Carnegie was a great believer in investing capital to improve his return. He profited greatly from investing heavily as a pioneer user of the Bessemer process of steel making. He saw that the public sector was not making enough investment in libraries, especially in smaller towns, and so was determined to fill the void.

4. Seeking Forgiveness for Homestead?

The tragic, bloody, deadly strike in 1892 at the Carnegie-controlled Homestead steel works remains a blot on American labor history. Ten or more people were killed in a day-long battle over an attempt to reduce wages by 18%. This was at a time when, by U.S. Department of Commerce figures, the average unskilled manufacturing wage earner was earning about 15 cents per hour for a work week of about 60 hours. While deep personal wounds remained, perhaps for life, it does not follow that Ohio's dozens of Carnegie libraries were in any way a plea for forgiveness.

5. Desire to die poor?

Andrew Carnegie once said that a man who dies rich dies disgraced, meaning that after the family was provided for, the rest of one's wealth should be devoted to the public good. Carnegie appeared to live by this aphorism, and, in fact, libraries were only a small part of his good works—about 13% by one tabulation.

Beyond Carnegie

Eventually, the Carnegie building boom reached what might be crudely called "saturation." Ohio's last Carnegie grant was $10,000 in 1915 to Ripley, a town in Brown County along the Ohio River that today has a population of around 2,000.

For this price, Ripley got one of the more interesting designs: the Prairie Style commonly associated with the eminent architect Frank

Lloyd Wright. It shuns the Greek Revival style common to so many Carnegie buildings in favor of red brick and a flattish red tile roof. It very much resembles Wright's well-known Unity Temple in Illinois. The connection could be more than coincidental, as the Ripley architect, a Mr. H.T. Liebert, came from Wright's native Wisconsin. A subsequent addition to the Ripley building in 1989 was carefully styled to retain Liebert's Prairie look. Note that the same Mr. Liebert also designed a Prairie Style structure for Milan, Ohio's Carnegie Library. By the time period of the last grant, the public library systems of all of Ohio's major cities had been well served by Mr. Carnegie's plan.

Some Major Ohio Library Buildings

Impressive progress was made in Ohio's library structure in spite of alternating periods of seeming affluence and recession that characterized the last half of the twentieth century. The following paragraphs profile three leaders: one in the north and one in the south, followed by a third in the center. The center-of-the-state example is the State Library of Ohio in Columbus. Their move to a recycled industrial building removed from the center of town hints at some trends for the future.

Cincinnati built a large book hall type library in 1874, based in buying a partially completed opera house. William Poole was librarian at the time of the 1874 Cincinnati building, which was in use until 1955. Subsequent replacements and additions to what became the main building of the Cincinnati and Hamilton County System were during the directorships of Carl Vitz (1955) and James Hunt (1982). The whole story of this pioneering 150-year-old major city library system is told in a new book *Free & Public* by nationally-known author and Cincinnati resident John Fleishman.

Cleveland's main, downtown library building was largely the work of long-time librarian William Brett (1846–1918), though he was killed in an accident long before its construction. His associate Linda Eastman (1867–1963) carried the project through to completion in 1925. Architects Walker and Weeks designed the classic revival structure following the Brett/Eastman program calling for subject departments and public access to most of the book collection. A $90 million bond issue financed major construction and renovation. The 1925 main building was completely and respectfully renovated in a $24 million project. A new adjoining building, The Louis Stokes Wing, was dedicated in 1997. It is a $65 million project of a striking semi-circular design, containing 267,000 square feet in eleven floors. A restored outdoor reading garden lies between the two buildings.

The State Library of Ohio is not a public library in the usual sense and therefore might not be considered for inclusion in this book. It is, however, public in another sense and some of its building issues are of interest here. SLO staff member Sandra Johnson researched the library's travels around Columbus since its beginning on December 25, 1817. The first location was in a building just north of the original State House. The initial book collection, received from Governor Thomas Worthington, was presided over by the first State librarian, John L. Harper. He was paid $2.00 per day—when the legislature was in session. In 1861, SLO moved to the present State House for a stay of seventy-two years. Still within a walkable circle around Capitol Square, SLO became an original tenant, in 1933, of the beautiful Ohio Departments Building at 65 South Front Street. Special quarters for SLO were provided on the top floor of this masterpiece of stonework and muraled interiors. The architect was Harry Hake of Cincinnati. Optimistic plans at the time were that all Ohio departments would fit within this one building.

Most recently, in 2000, space needs of another department forced the library to move to its fourth location. SLO is now at 274 East First Avenue, miles from the walk-in convenience of downtown Columbus. It is housed in a recycled heavy-industry manufacturing building. This seems like an unlikely situation for a library, but it has ample space for book storage, all needed electronic connections, and much simplified parking for visitors and staff. Other libraries with monumental buildings in congested areas may well rethink their strategy on location.

The Federal Side—In Briefly and Then Out

The Library Services and Construction Act (LSCA) was originally authorized by Congress in 1956 to extend public library service into rural areas. Eight years later, in 1964, Title II was added to support a measure of building construction. Finally, in 1966 Title III for Interlibrary Cooperation was added. The U.S. Department of Education became the responsible agency and the State Library of each state became the conduit and administrator. Here we will concentrate only on Title II, since its purpose was to build new buildings or remodel, expand, or otherwise improve buildings. These funds coming out of Title II had, albeit briefly, a large impact on library construction and, hence, the library service in the state.

In the first nine years of Title II's fractured life (1965–1974), a total of $7.3 million was contributed to the construction, remodeling, and equipping of fifty-eight public library buildings in thirty of Ohio's eighty-eight counties. This was only part of the financial story, since guidelines required that the local library had to invest a larger portion of the total cost—55% to the federal 45%. In the next nine years of Title II (1984–1993), forty-five buildings were improved with the federal input of $9.3 million. The final installment of federal funds under the on-again, off-again federal program was $2.9 million from 1994–1998 for just six buildings.

Fundamentally, the purpose of Title II was to extend and improve public library services, especially in less populated or otherwise undeserved areas. Some examples will illustrate what was done:
- In the early days, many embryonic public libraries found space in school buildings or store fronts. With an LSCA grant in 1989, the Martins Ferry Public Library was able to build a new branch and thereby extract itself from the local high school building. Five years later the storefront branch moved into its own building and installed its first telephone!
- Other de-bundling moves aided by Title II were in Newton Falls (from a school) and Caldwell, where in 1987 the library could finally leave the county courthouse for quarters of its own.

- A new main building was provided through a grant in 1990 to the Herbert Wescot Memorial Library in Vinton County.

With the nation moving increasingly on wheels rather than feet, parking space became almost as much of an issue as interior space. Some of the libraries that applied federal funds to their parking needs were: Samuel Bossard Memorial Library, Andover, the East Palestine Public Library, and the Champaign County Public Library in Urbana. Provision for meeting rooms or multi-purpose rooms were also often included in requests. This recognized the need for space for library-inspired programs and the role of libraries in accommodating community and civic groups.

During the LSCA period, the last half of the twentieth century, libraries became more than a collection of books and other material in print. Sound recordings, videos, and microfilms were added in large quantities. Special shelving was needed for these new forms and the equipment to store and use them. Copy machines, typewriters, and, yes, the first computer terminals were added.

Building Usage Changes

It is evident that the need to actually visit a public library is less now than in the pre-electronic age. Public libraries as buildings are competing among themselves and with what they make available to the home user. So far, that competition has been rather successful because libraries can claim excellent equipment and highly-trained staffs able to help the many customers who struggle with the computer back home.

Comparing some statistics for 1991 and 2001 from the Cleveland Heights-University Heights Public Library will illustrate. The number of people entering the library decreased 22% in the ten-year period. Further, the number of materials used in the library decreased 26%. Records of electronic usage have only been collected for recent years but what they show for just 2000 to 2001 is startling: a three-fold increase, and this covers access to and from the library, including some formerly nontraditional settings, i.e. home, school, office, college, etc.

All this added electronic activity has brought with it substantial increases in the space distribution for terminals, printers, and other behind-the-scenes equipment. Paradoxically, the usual indicator of library usage, circulation, shows that the number of items withdrawn has continued to grow by 36% in the past ten-year period. A major influence in the overall growth is the public's increased interest in audio-visual materials: up 148%. Conversion of space to accommodate the growing AV collection is of course required. DVDs are the current runaway favorite.

Summary

In 1803, "library," in most cases, meant a collection of books, and a floating collection at that. Usually small, these collections could be moved around easily as space was found. Some unusual locations for floating collections included a railroad station (Kent) and, in the case of Geneva, a private house—that of Platt R. Spencer, the father of American penmanship.

Andrew Carnegie, industrialist turned philanthropist, financed the construction of over one hundred buildings in Ohio to house those floating collections of books. By this means, a "library" became a place. A destination. By the end of the Carnegie program in 1920, Carnegie buildings graced the small towns, neighborhoods, and city centers of Ohio, thereby establishing the concept of a library as a freestanding, proud community resource.

Responding to local demand, library systems have built branches in areas of population growth. Private gifts and grants have often assisted. Most building funds are locally derived and controlled, but federal funds played a part during eighteen years between the sixties and the nineties.

The arrival of electronic online resources has resulted in a profound revolution in the way libraries are used. Many needs for information are now met by the library via the home computer. But still they keep coming to borrow materials, use the terminals, question the staff, or to use the building as a community center. Now, perhaps more than ever, the library is a place for films, lectures, and community meetings. It's one of Ohio's proudest, most cherished institutions.

The Sandusky Library: A Case Study

—Barbara Bishop
Development Coordinator, Sandusky Library

The Sandusky Library was incorporated in 1895, through the efforts of a group of dedicated women who wanted to build a library in the heart of downtown Sandusky, Ohio, on the Lake Erie coast. Mrs. Jay O. Moss, the group's leader, solicited a generous donation of $50,000 from Andrew Carnegie. Mr. Carnegie's gift was contingent upon the city's contribution of $3,000 annually to maintain the building. The city was delighted to accept the terms of Mr. Carnegie's gift, and the feeling of the community was conveyed in the headline of the *Sandusky Register*, November 8, 1899, which read, "What the Ladies Have Worked for is Now Assured."

One of the first Carnegie libraries in Ohio, Sandusky Library was a vital community center that housed a growing book collection, a music hall, and the historical society. Today, the books have taken over the entire building and two branches. The historical society room has grown into the library's Follett House Museum, located two blocks east of the central library. The recitals and lectures once held in the music hall are now sponsored by the library's Lange Trust in auditoriums around the city. The library the ladies envisioned one hundred years ago is the same in mission and scope, only larger in scale.

Today we are building a "new" library, a project the community has embraced with the same enthusiasm, determination, and love for the library they demonstrated so long ago. The Sandusky Library expansion and renovation is a unique undertaking, aimed at preserving two of the city's architectural treasures. The existing Carnegie Library, built in 1901, is being joined to the former Erie County Jail, built in 1883 on property adjacent to the library. The two National Historic Register buildings are being integrated into one modern facility, with new space added to the back of the buildings, and in the space between. The new library will preserve the architectural integrity of the beautiful old buildings, but will nearly triple in size to 62,000 square feet, with all of the benefits of modern technology, accessibility for the disabled, and other amenities for today's library patrons.

Sandusky voters approved a $7.2 million bond issue in 1998 to cover the basic construction and architectural fees for the project. The library's foundation raised additional private dollars for property purchases, equipment, computers, furnishings, and construction and architectural upgrades for the new facility. With the generous support of the community, the fundraising goal was reached. The headline of the *Lorain Morning Journal* on October 3, 2002, once again reflected the feeling of the community and read, "Library Ready to Close Book on Campaign, Happy Ending: Sandusky Library officials report $3 million in gifts."

An Early Library Building: A Case Study
—H. Baird Tenney and Rachel Wayne Nelson

A library building was erected in Ohio's statehood year, 1803, in Worthington, now a northern suburb of Columbus. The community was planned to accommodate pioneers willing to leave their Connecticut homes for the relative wilds of what would be the state of Ohio.

From the start, a library was part of the plan, to be set on the village green in the center of town. It was to be placed in a log structure on a $1^1/_2$ acre segment of the east side of the village green. The building also housed the first school. The location was on Main Street, now High Street, and with a stretch of the historical imagination might have carried the same street number, 820, as today's Worthington Library.

Officially, the library came to life December 23, 1803, when bylaws were signed and Zophar Topping was chosen to "Keep & take Care of the Library Belonging to this Company." This was not a public, tax-supported library, but rather a subscription library, with certain payments expected from users. Subscription libraries were the norm for frontier communities if a community was to have any type of library at all. Most did not.

Enter the ADA: A Case Study
—H. Baird Tenney and Rachel Wayne Nelson

During the 1960s and 1970s librarians became aware that there were library customers and potential workers who could not navigate those glorious front steps of the typical Carnegie building in a wheelchair. Congress listened and decided people with disabilities have their own brand of civil rights and passed the ADA (Americans with Disabilities Act).

Seen as landmark federal anti-discrimination legislation, the ADA ensures equal access to employment opportunities, state and local government, private commercial facilities that offer goods, services, and activities to the public, transportation, and telecommunications for people with disabilities.

Public librarians were not too surprised by ADA since they have long understood that their mission is to be open to and serve all comers. Federal funds were an obvious aid in solving some of the problems of accessibility. Many projects to provide elevators, ramps, powered doors, and barrier-free restrooms soon followed. And some of these special features turned out to aid the flow of general users too.

Where's that Card Catalog?
—H. Baird Tenney and Rachel Wayne Nelson

It was during the LSCA Title II period that the venerable card catalog became a very real technical and human issue. From the 1970s, great progress was made in computerization. The online catalog and specialized databases were relentlessly moving to replace the iconic card catalog as the information engine and physical center of the library. Space needs would require much reconfiguration to make way for multiple access terminals.

Reaction to this loss or displacement of the card catalog initially was surprise, disappointment, and often hostility. Claims that the online catalog was more efficient, more versatile, and more up-to-date and able to access other library collections often fell on deaf ears. For an extended period, it fell to the staff to teach, empathize, and literally hold the hand of customers anguished by the disappearance of their beloved card catalog.

Clear Heads, Strong Hands, and Great Hearts: The Staff of Ohio's Libraries
HARRIET CLEM and MARGARET ALBRIGHT

For over 150 years, Ohio public librarians have taken pride in their libraries, served the public impartially, and at times, placed the library above their own personal benefit. Ohio's librarians are the force behind the state's library excellence. There are far too many to name, but there are several that stand out as giants in Ohio's early library history, including Charles B. Galbreath, Electra C. Doren, William Howard Brett, Herbert S. Hirshberg, and Linda A. Eastman. These were the librarians who acquired, preserved, and organized the documents and materials of Ohio's libraries. These were the men and women who invented librarianship, providing the foundation for some of the best library systems in the country.

I. Outstanding Librarians

William Howard Brett

Innovator, always accessible, a true book lover, one of the biggest men in the profession, a fair and able administrator, lover of justice and tolerance, kind-hearted, possessor of rare good judgment, counselor. These are just a few of the descriptions given of William Howard Brett, director of the Cleveland Public Library from 1884 to 1918. His insistence on providing space and materials for children also earned him the title, "greatest children's librarian."

Brett was known as a knowledgeable bookseller in Cleveland; however, he had no formal library training. No doubt the library board's decision to hire Brett was a sound one, for Brett became one of the most beloved and respected of Ohio's librarians. All of those who knew Brett, or read of him, would agree that his first consideration always was successfully serving patrons and making the library easier for the general public to use. In the late nineteenth century, he was the first director of a large metropolitan library to introduce the open shelf, allowing patrons access to the collection. His trust in people was well founded; fewer books were lost in the year following the introduction of the open shelf policy, while circulation had doubled.

Organization of the library was paramount to ease of use; therefore, Brett published his own dictionary catalogue in 1889, modeled after Electra Doren's catalogue for the Dayton Public Library, and he adopted the new Dewey Decimal System with some amendments. Brett organized Cleveland's main library into subject departments, enabling the staff to become specialists in individual areas, with the consequent improvement in answering reference questions and ordering books.

By 1896, in order to keep the contents of periodicals accessible, Brett had begun publishing his monthly "Cumulative Index to a Selected List of Periodicals" (encompassing 100 periodicals), which he offered to other libraries for their use. Brett's index was later merged with the less comprehensive H.W. Wilson's *Reader's Guide to Periodical Literature*.

William Howard Brett was not content to improve Cleveland's library, but also sought to bring the library to more people. He opened extensions in schools, children's homes, stores, and firehouses. His branch library system extended to all areas, and his work with Andrew Carnegie in library design and use led to Brett publishing his *Abstract of Laws Relating to Libraries in Force in the States and Territories of the United States* in 1916.

Brett was the dean of the School of Library Science at Western Reserve University for fourteen years, having helped to establish the school in 1904. The Cleveland Public Library's training classes for children's librarians became a specialized course later on at the library school.

Making space available for children was important to Brett, and he was able to open a children's room in 1898, and provide a trained children's librarian. Love of people and love of books was apparent in William Howard Brett, and he inspired his staff and the general public as well. To provide an illustration, we quote Brett's successor at the Cleveland Public Library, Linda Eastman, writing in *Portrait of a Librarian*, American Library Association, 1940: "The rather timid young girl ... had gone one day to the library for a book which was required reading in her school course, and just as she was being told by the assistant that the book was not in, Mr. Brett came through the gate in the counter. Perhaps the disappointment registered on the face of the young borrower attracted his sympathetic attention, for he stepped over to her and said, 'If you care to wait about twenty minutes, I'll send right down to the bookstore and get another copy of the book for you.'"

Electra C. Doren

As an assistant at the Dayton Public Library, Electra Doren published a dictionary book catalog in 1881. It was only the fourth of its kind in the United States. This catalog was read by William Howard Brett in Cleveland, and it influenced the compilation of his own. Before the twentieth century had begun, Electra Doren, as director of the Dayton Public Library, had adopted an open shelf policy, opened a children's room in the main library, began working in schools, and formed an apprentice training class that was the second one in the nation. In 1903, she established four deposit stations in schools.

Electra Doren lectured at the Carnegie Library School in Pittsburgh, and was the first director of the Western Reserve University Library School. Returning to Dayton in 1913, she helped rebuild the library's collection after the flood. In 1923, she began the state's first city bookmobile service. Doren served at Dayton Public Library until her death in 1927, having always looked to the future with intelligence, and laying a firm and broad foundation for the Dayton Public Library.

Linda A. Eastman

Successor to William Howard Brett at the Cleveland Public Library, Linda Eastman was the only woman director of a large metropolitan library. She also was the only female Ohio public librarian elected to honorary membership in the American Library Association. Along with Brett, Eastman helped to organize the library school at Western Reserve and taught there for thirty-four years. She helped found the Ohio Library Association with Brett and Electra Doren.

Continuing the extension work of Brett, Eastman opened service to hospitals and factories, as well as the homebound and the blind. The Business Information Bureau organized under Eastman in 1928 was recognized as one of the most comprehensive in the country. Equally impressive was the travel section, growing from a pamphlet file in 1926 to an entire room by the 1970s, and arguably the best in the world.

Linda Eastman planned and supervised two complete moves of the Cleveland Public Library, the first in 1913 and the second in 1925, to its permanent home. After this latter move to Superior Avenue, the Cleveland Public Library became the third largest library in the United States. Only the New York Public Library and the Library of Congress are larger, and those two are not as functional or well-equipped. Certainly this library, planned by William Howard Brett and Linda Eastman, was built with the library patron in mind.

Charles B. Galbreath

Charles Galbreath, born in Ohio and lifelong resident of our state, held the position of State Librarian two times, from 1896 to 1911, and from 1915 to 1918. His first term began in the year that the State Library Board of Commissions became a little less politicized, with the governor of Ohio appointing three citizens to the board, and neither the governor nor his fellow office holders were members. Now it became more likely that the State Librarian would be chosen on the basis of his abilities, and Charles Galbreath proved himself worthy.

Trained and experienced in education, Galbreath graduated from Mount Union College in Alliance in 1882, and received Bachelor of

Philosophy, Bachelor of Commercial Science, and Bachelor of Arts degrees, as well as Master of Arts in 1894. Galbreath had been superintendent of schools in Wilmot, Ohio, and in East Palestine, and president of Mt. Hope College in Rogers, Ohio. Charles Galbreath's five-volume *History of Ohio* is recognized nationwide, and his poem, "In Flanders Fields, An Answer," shows his loyalty and sense of duty even as he followed his Quaker devotion to nonviolence.

As State Librarian, Galbreath endeavored to open service to all persons and to reach remote areas of the state. He sent boxes of books to various locations, and thus began his innovative traveling libraries, which soon became the largest system in the nation. The "Galbreath Collection" was his accumulation of Ohio newspapers. He was always ready to assist small libraries and to help with new libraries. Galbreath also was able to classify the library's collection and create a shelf list. He published the first newsletter about the State Library and other Ohio libraries.

From 1927 to 1928, Charles Galbreath voluntarily served as Acting State Librarian rather than see the library close due to lack of appropriations by the state legislature. His dedication was beyond question, not just as State Librarian, but also as writer and educator.

Herbert Simon Hirshberg

The first professional librarian to lead the State Library was Herbert Hirshberg, who also had extensive library experience before coming to Ohio. Hirshberg had worked at the Library of Congress and the Carnegie Library in Pittsburgh. He had been a reference librarian at the Cleveland Public Library and also taught at Western Reserve Library School. As the director of the Toledo Public Library, Hirshberg opened the first branch library in 1915 and oversaw the building of five Carnegie-financed branches. By 1919, sixty percent of Toledo's circulation was done at the branches.

Arriving at the State Library, Hirshberg began expanding the library's services to all state residents. He added to the traveling libraries to reach more rural areas, worked with school libraries extensively, and established the county library system in Ohio.

Though only director at the Akron Public Library for a short time, Herbert Hirshberg provided one of the most valuable assets to the library and the city of Akron by hiring "the Story Lady," Harriet Leaf, for the children's department.

Hirshberg spent the remainder of his library career as dean of the School of Library Science at Western Reserve University. Simultaneously, he was the Director of Libraries at Western Reserve, where he established the Union Catalog for the use of Cleveland, university, and college libraries.

II. Other Notable Librarians

Librarians who were pioneers in new libraries or contributed new ideas, methods, or services were numerous in Ohio, and deserve more than this mention, and also our thanks for their unselfish service to library patrons. A partial list would include Margaret E. Wright Thayer, Amy Winslow, and Lewis Naylor of the Cuyahoga County Public Library, Mary Pauline Edgerton, Maude Herndon, and R. Russell Munn of Akron Public Library, Mary P. Martin of the Canton Public Library, Clarence W. Sumner and James C. Foutts of Youngstown Public Library, William James Hamilton, and William Chait of Dayton Public Library, Rose Vormelker, Marilla Freeman, Donna Root, and Raymond C. Lindquist of the Cleveland Public Library, Chalmers Hadley and N.D. Carlile Hodges of the Cincinnati Public Library, and Robert D. Franklin of the Toledo Public Library.

Ohio has been fortunate enough to be home to excellent children's librarians: those who worked to see that children were provided space and materials of their own, and those who developed quality children's departments. Effie L. Power (1873–1969) began her library career in 1895 at Cleveland Public Library. William Howard Brett appointed her to be in charge of the library's first children's room. Power's contributions to children's work included the training of children's librarians and teaching methodology and children's literature at Cleveland's City Normal School. Effie Power was primarily responsible for the training class at Cleveland Public Library that she helped to develop into a graduate program at Western Reserve University School of Library

Science. Her text, *Library Service for Children*, was the first on the subject and was used nationwide in training classes and library schools.

Ruth M. Hadlow spent her entire library career at Cleveland Public Library, working with the city's children for over fifty years. A great storyteller, Ruth Hadlow read to children in the library, in schools, and on the radio. She encouraged reading aloud by families also, stressing the importance of fostering both intimacy and imagination. Hadlow collaborated on some editions of *Children's Books Too Good to Miss*, assisted with the year-end list of recommended children's books published by the Cleveland Public Library, and was a member of the Newberry-Caldecott Award Committee.

Ohio's pioneering librarians learned the library trade as they worked and as they trained and mentored others, and they shared the knowledge gained with their peers. How did succeeding generations learn librarianship, and how did library work become a recognized profession? What kind of staff developed in Ohio's libraries? Who are today's librarians?

III. Professional Staff Development

To my thinking, a great librarian must have a clear head, a strong hand, and above all, a great heart ... and I am inclined to think that most of the men who will achieve this greatness will be *women*. [italics added]
—Melvil Dewey

This prediction from the father of librarianship was borne out in the staffing at many Ohio public libraries, and the nation as well. The following information from Rodman Public Library in Alliance is likely to be typical of other medium and small libraries in Ohio. For the first twenty-three years of its infancy, the Rodman Library had ten library directors. Of the ten, nine were women. This picture was probably repeated in most smaller public libraries of that era (1900–1923). Three of the women began as "single ladies" and left employment after they married. The first "trained" library director assumed her position in 1912, after completing one year of training at The University of Chicago.

Of Ohio's 250 public libraries, 183 now have librarians with an American Library Association accredited Master of Library Science degree (U.S. Dept. of Education, Public Libraries Survey, 2000). Many decades of Ohio public library history passed before this degree of professionalism was evident among the staff. There were early library schools in the nineteenth century, and in-house training classes were disseminating knowledge among the staff. Pinpointing when changes in the education of staff began is difficult due to a lack of data, and also to differences in the definitions of "professional" and "librarian." In a 1967 survey of Ohio public libraries by Philip Ennis, six percent of the "professional" staff of Ohio's largest libraries had no college degree. For this survey, the head librarian of each library decided which of the staff were professionals. In Ohio's smallest libraries, sixty-five percent of those considered professionals had no college degree, and only three percent held a master's degree. This report also showed that male librarians were much more likely to have attained an MLS or higher degree than were female librarians.

Reports and surveys of staff characteristics are more numerous today, but research in 1904 by Salome Cutler Fairchild was an unusual early inquiry into the status of women and men in American libraries. Fairchild found that men held the top administrative positions in all but the smallest public libraries, and also that male administrators earned higher salaries than female administrators—dramatically higher in the largest libraries. Nationally, these statistics were confirmed in studies by Alice Bryan in 1952, Anita Schiller in 1974, and again by Kathleen Heim in 1982.

The Ennis report of 1967 confirmed that in Ohio, men were more likely to hold the position of head librarian in large libraries. However, in Ohio's largest libraries, eighty-eight percent of the librarians were female. In 1959, of Ohio's nine metropolitan libraries, eight of the nine had male directors; in 2002, the same is true. Cincinnati is the only library of the nine to be headed by a woman. In addition, every state librarian of Ohio has been male except for a brief period in the 1960s when Ruth Hess was acting state librarian. Nevertheless, when considering all administrative positions in all public libraries in Ohio, including directors, assistant directors, and department heads, the overwhelming majority are women. Some analysts have surmised that the job description of the top position in large libraries is simply too far removed from the idea of librarianship for most of those choosing a library career.

The American Library Association, in the November 1998 *American Libraries*, published the results of a questionnaire covering a national sample of academic and public librarians. In public libraries in the United States, 78.91% of employees are female. Total minority employment in public libraries is 13.45%, with African-American librarians comprising almost half of that total. Although there is no comparable study for Ohio in that year, a 1991 report by Alan Rees and Rosemary DuMont shows Ohio statistics similar to the national figures. *Study of Library Human Resources in Ohio Libraries* reports 87% of public librarians to be female, and a total minority employment in public libraries of Ohio at 10.77%, of which 9.99% are African-American. Improving employment opportunities for minorities in Ohio is recommended in the study, as it has been nationally. Cleveland Public Library now has its first African-American director. Andrew Venable was named director in 1999, responsible for the third largest library system in the country. Reminiscent of William Howard Brett, Venable calls the library the "people's university" and has said he will work to increase use of all aspects of the library. Widening the breadth of diversity in Ohio library staff should be a worthy goal and is recognized by library schools. Surely those who choose a library career know that Ohio has an excellent educational facility in Kent State School of Library and Information Science.

How did professional training develop in Ohio? Despite the fact that Ohio was home to only two schools of library science accredited by the American Library Association, Dayton Public Library had established a library training school that was the second one in the United States. Dayton's director, Electra Doren, recognized the need for more education of library employees and in 1896, her first year as head of the library, she began the Dayton Training School. Doren, a well-respected innovator, was asked by William Howard Brett to become the first director of the Western Reserve University Library School.

Brett, convinced of the need for professional training among his Cleveland Public Library staff, and in the same year that Electra Doren was beginning her training school, brought the University of Chicago's extension course in library work to the main library. Virtually all of the staff attended. Two years later he hired Electra Doren to teach summer classes in librarianship. There were twice as many applications for the class than expected, including those from other states. With the aid of Charles Thwing, President of Case Western Reserve University, Brett secured $100,000 from Andrew Carnegie to fund a library school. By 1904 Brett had his library school, Case Western Reserve Library School, with a first-year attendance of twenty-nine students. Over the years, the School of Library Science was housed in six different locations. The last building, from 1974 until 1986, being on the same site as was the university's original Hatch Library built in 1896.

William Brett was dean of the school until his death in 1918. His first director was Electra Doren, no doubt an excellent choice for the position. However, due to ill health, she was only able to serve for two years. Julia Whittlesey succeeded Doren in 1906, and Alice Tyler became director in 1913. Tyler worked to improve the school and its curriculum. By 1927, the school was able to award its first Bachelor of Science in Library Science, requiring four years of college and one year of library training. Tyler also brought new programs to the school: special courses in hospital service and work in special libraries, a program for children's librarians under the direction of Effie Power, and a specialization for school librarians supervised by Annie Cutter. In 1925, Alice Tyler became dean of the library school, filling the vacancy left since Brett's death in 1918.

In 1929, Herbert Hirshberg became director of the library school and by 1935 was able to obtain graduate status for all programs, having complied with the standards established by the American Library Association Board of Education for Librarianship. Hirshberg also introduced the master's degree program in library service for children in 1930. Although an excellent program, six years later it was discontinued due to its expense and the scarcity of students. The Great Depression had a serious effect on the finances of the school. Loans and scholarships were reduced, income from investments plummeted, and the school became seriously indebted to banks.

Western Reserve made a turnaround under Thirza Grant, who saw the enrollment increase from an average of eighty-five students per year to 174 per year. The 1940s saw a severe shortage of library personnel, and library schools all over the nation were filled to capacity. The decade of the forties also saw improved accreditation standards, and more uniformity in curriculum among library schools. At Western Reserve, Thirza Grant adopted a new program for the master's degree, increasing the requirements in hours and courses. By 1948, the Master of Science in Library Science was offered, and Grant offered this degree to those who had the Bachelor of Science in Library Science, provided they complete twenty-one hours of graduate school courses. Emphasis was now placed on bibliography and reference, literature in wide subject areas, research, and evaluation of resources. True graduate education had arrived and the apprentice program abandoned. Accreditation for the program followed.

Jesse Hauk Shera was dean at Western Reserve from 1952 to 1970. Shera helped to develop a curriculum for a doctoral program which was established by 1959, and was the first in the country to combine study in librarianship with other fields such as science, humanities, or social studies, and dissertation requirements were the same as for any other doctoral program at the university.

Shera also expanded course offerings for school librarians, introduced new courses in law librarianship, library architecture, photographic techniques, music librarianship, and archives. In 1967, Jesse Shera was also responsible for introducing the first program in the country leading to a master's degree in Medical Librarianship and Health Science Information. Undoubtedly, Shera's major accomplishment that would help pave the road to the future of information retrieval was his Center for Documentation and Communication Research.

Under Shera and his successor, William Goffman, the academic standing of the faculty of Case Western Reserve Library School increased in quality, and in 1975 the American Library Association ranked the school first in the United States and Canada in faculty research. The ALA also ranked the school first in the amount of money it made available for financial assistance, and thus was able to attract many foreign students. The School of Library Science in Cleveland had a remarkable history of achievements and was home to many successful faculty and students. Its decreasing endowment forced its closure in 1986.

The School of Library and Information Sciences at Kent State University began as a department in the College of Education in 1946. As a graduate program, the first degrees were conferred in 1950. American Library Association accreditation was granted in 1963.

Kent's library school maintains a Center for the Study of Librarianship to accept funding for research. The center was begun in 1966 with aid from the State Library of Ohio. For almost twenty-five years, the library school operated its Center for the Study of Ethnic Publications and Cultural Institutions in the United States. In 1975, Kent offered courses in Columbus, cooperating with Ohio State University. This program has been so successful that by the late 1980s full-time faculty was needed.

The School of Library Science at Kent opened its first computer lab in 1986, and has continued to make available to its students the technological advancements necessary for library work today. In 1991, the school's name was changed to the School of Library and Information Science. Today's library students are able to participate in Kent's new distance education program, enabling students to take most of their course work via interactive video. Also available is the Master of Science in Information Architecture and Knowledge Management. Updating skills is recognized as vital today, and Kent State SLIS offers a sixth-year Certificate of Advanced Study.

Kent State SLIS will be an important part of the future for Ohio's librarians. Ohio has fine librarians, willing to mentor those who will follow. The future may be quite different than can be imagined. However, the vision of a great librarian will not change, and Ohio has both men and women who have Dewey's "clear head, strong hand, and great heart."

Burton Stevenson: A Case Study

—Jennifer Thompson

He was an internationally known figure in his day, and his obituary appeared in the *New York Times, Time,* and *Newsweek* when he died. He authored over fifty books, two of which were made into movies. An expatriate and gourmet, he lived for years in Paris. Who was he? He was the librarian from Chillicothe, Ohio—Burton Stevenson.

On February 12, 2003, an Ohio Historical Marker in honor of Stevenson was dedicated at the Chillicothe and Ross County Public Library. That library is the successor to the Chillicothe Public Library where, incredibly, Stevenson was the librarian for fifty-eight years, from 1899 to 1957. Incredible because during that time period he also wrote or compiled all those books, started a troop library at Camp Sherman that became a model for all others during World War I, served as the European director of the Library War Service, and founded the American Library in Paris. The American Library in Paris became a model for all subsequent libraries organized by the United States Information Service and is still in existence today. While he was in Europe during World War I, and later during his tenure at the American Library from 1918–20 and 1925–30, he was on leave of absence from the Chillicothe Public Library, kept running by loyal assistants.

The Stevenson book probably most recognized by librarians is the *Home Book of Quotations.* Stevenson was known for compiling numerous anthologies of quotations and poetry, a laborious job in those pre-computer days. He wrote a tremendous amount of fiction as well, mostly adventure stories and books for young people. *The Mystery of the Boule Cabinet* and *The Little Comrade* were the two that became movies. His books were translated into many languages. Perhaps Stevenson's most striking personal characteristic is that he was hugely productive.

A collection of Stevenson's works, his correspondence, and memorabilia are on permanent display at the Chillicothe and Ross County Public Library.

Chapman Parsons

A chapter listing his accomplishments could easily be written about A. Chapman Parsons. He completed eight years as director of the Rodman Public Library in Alliance leaving in 1964 to become the first executive director of the newly founded Ohio Library Association/Ohio Library Trustees Association. He retired from that position in 1987 and died in 1994. The organization later became the Ohio Library Council.

Serving Every Citizen: Ohio's Library Patrons, Outreach Services, and Friends Groups

MELINDA F. HILL

Ohio's libraries wouldn't be anything without the people they serve. Ohio's first library "patrons" were the pioneers who first settled here, who felt their lives wouldn't be complete without a selection of books from back East. Today, Ohio's library patrons are its entire population. Incredibly diverse, Ohio has bustling urban centers and acres of farmland, the affluent and the poor, lifelong residents and new immigrants. Libraries are a reflection of the communities they serve, and this chapter will chronicle some of the changes and challenges libraries have met as the population they serve has changed. It will also address one of the most direct ways patrons support libraries—Friends of the Library groups.

The First Patrons

The first library "patrons" were, not too surprisingly, some of the first residents of Ohio. The first library was started by a group of New Englanders in Belpre, Ohio. Belpre was part of a land purchase by the Ohio Company of Associates in 1787. Although sweeping generalizations can be a dangerous thing, we do know that most of the settlers were former officers in the Continental Army who were willing to give up monetary security for the opportunities afforded by settling a new land. Mark Neyman, author of the article "The First Library in Ohio" in the October 1976 *Ohio Library Association Bulletin*, quotes Judge Barker as saying "Some of them had been liberally educated, and all had received the advantages of common schools in early life. ..." Although education was an important part of their lives, that took a back seat to the primary concern of survival during the first years of settlement in Belpre. After a few years of settlement, though, Colonel Israel Putnam, recently returned from the Indian Wars, formed the first circulating library in Ohio, the Putnam Family Library, in 1796.

Free libraries are something taken fairly for granted today. Most early libraries, though, were subscription, which involved buying of shares and possibly an annual tax for upkeep and purchase of materials. The Putnam Family Library was subscription, as was the famed Coonskin Library, which was opened to shareholders on February 2, 1804. This was a group of settlers much like the ones who settled in Belpre. The families settled near Athens, starting in 1797. The community grew quickly over the next few years. Interest in educational matters can be seen as early as 1801, when parents secured the services of a teacher, Moses Everett. Reading materials were difficult to come by. "It is true that Ephraim Cutler [one of the first settlers] took the *United States Gazette* published in Philadelphia, but that 'except by fortunate accident did not arrive much oftener than once in three months,' and being by no means even a sixteen page issue, the numbers hardly sufficed for the intellectual food of the settlement, though it was loaned far and wide with the liberality of pioneer custom" says Sarah J. Cutler in an article from the *Ohio Archeological and Historical Society Publications*. With the rigors involved in travel at the time, few books were brought with them, so the family Bible and the very occasional *Gazette* were what got them by. These offerings alone, though, didn't satisfy them, and talk began of a library.

But how to get books? Money was quite scarce, as noted by A.G. Brown in Cutler's article: "So scarce was money that I can hardly remember ever seeing a piece of coin till I was a well-grown boy. It was with difficulty that we obtained enough to pay our taxes and buy tea for Mother. As for clothes and other things, we either depended on the forests for them, or bartered for them, or did without" (Cutler, 63). They decided to combine what money they had with skins to sell.

These were taken to Boston. Books were purchased and brought back, and the library was started in 1804.

While it's easy to wax romantic about the early settlers of Ohio and their "bronzed faces and toilworn hands, toughened in sinew by wielding the axe and saw ... wearing their everyday homespun and buckskin garments" (Cutler, 62), the truth of the matter is they were clearly people who wanted to bring the best of what they had known in the East into the Northwest Territory with them. While they were breaking new ground and starting new lives, they desired education for their children and quality entertainment during the winter months for themselves. This desire led to the founding of two to three subscription libraries within the first years of Ohio's settlement, an impressive statement of the desires of the first Westerners to begin a good life anew.

While the desire to have books available is admirable, the "free library" we take for granted today was still a long way off. Belpre and the Coonskin Library set a "precedent for some 187 other 'social' libraries established throughout Ohio prior to 1850" (Blasingame, 16). These social libraries operated much like the schools of the time: they were open to anyone who could afford the subscription fee. Undoubtedly, this left out some settlers who could not afford the fee. Some libraries, such as the Coonskin, would accept trades rather than money, and this expanded the scope of those who could take advantage of library services.

As the population of Ohio grew during the 1820s and 1830s, new libraries developed that catered to different classes—apprentice or mechanic libraries and mercantile libraries, one of which is still operating in Cincinnati today. These libraries "appealed to young men of lower to middle class background" (Blasingame, 18) and were usually supported by subscriptions paid by the workers.

Over the course of the nineteenth century, libraries were frequently established through bequests. The Wells Library, for example, was founded in 1860 through a bequest from Henry Wells, an Albany, Ohio, merchant. Regretting his lack of formal education, he left $250 for the purchase of books and $1000 to endow the library. These books were housed in the Masonic Hall. The Elyria Public Library was similarly funded from the estate of Charles A. Ely, opening in 1870. With these libraries, a broader scope of people were able to take advantage of library service. Libraries were viewed as a community asset, rather than simply an asset to those with the means to subscribe.

An editorial in the October 1, 1880, *Youngstown Vindicator* by the executive committee of the Youngstown Library Association expresses the community desire to have more books that could be loaned to families with children in school. "No education force is making its presence felt to any greater extent than our library. No one can estimate what it has done towards creating a taste for useful reading. Its grand aim is to supplant the reading of the pernicious literature so much read by our children, and to place in its stead the choicest works on all subjects to be found in the English language. ... No boy, who is a constant reader of good books, can do a mean, low act." The Youngstown Library was formally incorporated a few weeks after the editorial appeared.

Making Public Libraries Truly Public

In 1890, William Howard Brett started the open shelf system in Cleveland. This was the first metropolitan library to do so. The implications of an open shelf system are really immeasurable; after all, going into a library and perusing the shelves is taken for granted today. C.H. Cramer, author of *Open Shelves, Open Minds*, a history of the Cleveland Public Library, describes Brett's reasons for allowing the public physical access to the books: "Brett supported the open shelf because of his faith in humankind and his belief that borrowers from libraries must be presented with the maximum of choice ... he realized that borrowers in libraries must be relieved of the high counters, which were formidable barriers, if a real choice was to be offered to them." Before the open shelf system, borrowers had a list of titles and had to submit a call slip to have the book pulled for them. It is easy to see how intimidating this might be for someone not familiar with book titles, or with books in general. It was a major shift in thinking for libraries, and immensely freeing for the public. Cramer explains: "Because a public library was founded on the principle of generosity and helpfulness, [Brett] felt that narrowing and hampering rules were foreign, repugnant, and ineffective."

Brett also started shelving the nonfiction books by subject, a system modeled after Electra C. Doren's dictionary catalog, then a radical departure from shelving all books by author. He also put together a catalog that could be understood by the public as well as librarians, also fairly unusual. Brett was key in making the public library truly public, with books accessible in every possible way. The results are still seen today, with libraries using the Dewey Decimal System and catalogs readily available via computer. It was a move from libraries as protectors of books to providers of books. All patrons, regardless of education, could come in and peruse the shelves for exactly what they were looking for, without intimidation.

Public accessibility to libraries was even more improved with the founding of the Brumback Library. This was the first county library in the world. It was started in Van Wert County in 1899 by John Sanford Brumback. Brumback, like Brett, felt that books should be in easy reach of as many people as possible. He gave the first county library to the citizens of Van Wert and it was a pioneer in providing library service to rural areas. Until then, many libraries were organized by school district, or were still available by subscription only. To have books available to all residents of a county was an exciting, and undoubtedly nerve-racking, endeavor. It made Ohio libraries what they are today, however: freely available to all residents of Ohio, regardless of race or income.

Patrons of the Twentieth Century

Through the twentieth century, Ohio libraries continued to improve service to all population groups. Libraries provided respite from the strain of the depression of the 1930s. Cramer quotes Linda Eastman saying: "Many of the librarians have been told by wives taking out many books, 'If I didn't have these, I don't know what we'd do. They're the only things which saved my husband's reason. At least they give him something to do. He has a chance to forget himself.'" The first half of the twentieth century was marked by war, and libraries provided services to those affected. Lorain Library, during World War II, served as a War Information Center, provided technical books for industrial defense workers, helped maintain civilian morale by interpreting current facts and events, and relieved the strain of war by providing recreational reading for men, women, and especially children. They also hired women bookmobile drivers when it was difficult to find men during the war.

Libraries Without Walls

Ohio's library services have extended far beyond its walls and those inside them, however. Early on, Ohio librarians recognized that there were populations that were greatly in need of library service, but weren't able to come to the building. Branch libraries opened, but there were still people that couldn't take advantage of library services. So the library went to them. Outreach programs began to bring services to the homebound, the disabled, and the incarcerated. Libraries met the need for additional library materials in schools by lending out classroom collections and buying bookmobiles to bring even more books to them. Libraries began programming to bring in new ethnic populations and migrant workers, adding books in their native language to collections, and beginning English as a Second Language classes to help them adapt to their new home. Libraries began services to meet the needs of the blind and deaf. Libraries adapted, and found new ways to provide services to the populations they served. Ohio has been extraordinarily innovative in the ways it has reached out to extend the library beyond its walls.

One of the primary places Ohio libraries have reached out to is the state's schools. Frequently school library book budgets are tight, and staff time is even tighter. Public libraries have been partnering with schools in different ways since the late 1800s, beginning with Cleveland Public Library in 1884. Cleveland Public began issuing teacher's cards, giving the holder the right to draw up to five books at a time (at that time, patrons could usually only have one book out of the library at a time). This was the first Ohio library to extend this privilege and the second library in the country. In 1887, Cleveland Public sent its first collection of books to a classroom and called it a "classroom library." Columbus followed suit in 1892, purchasing a few hundred books called "Classics for Children" and loaning them to schools in blocks of twenty-five. In 1896, Cleveland opened the first high school library branch in Central High School.

Public libraries have also maintained a presence in schools through classroom visits. A 1979 Survey of Children's Services conducted by the State Library of Ohio showed public librarians spending an average of two to five hours per month in the classroom. Programming ranges from presenting basic library services and library card applications to, today, teaching teen parents how to read to their children. Although few libraries have branches in schools today, many are utilizing bookmobiles to take the library to the school.

The first bookmobile in the United States was in Hagerstown, Maryland, in 1905. Dayton was the first city in Ohio to purchase a book wagon in 1923, at the extravagant cost of $623.04. The first book trailer was purchased by Clark County in 1933 to provide services to area small towns. Their bookmobile service continues today, stopping everywhere from preschools to apartment complexes to Young's Dairy Farm near Yellow Springs. The State Library established a traveling library department in 1896. Its first visit was to a women's club in Mount Vernon. In 1956, the State Library established bookmobile programs from funds made available from the Library Services Act. In 1958, The State Library board initiated the first six of its planned Regional Service Centers. By the 1970s, twenty-two counties were being given subsidized service contracts for their bookmobile service. Today, bookmobiles utilize wireless technology to allow the bookmobile to truly serve as another branch, with catalog card access and the ability to request materials from other locations. As of 2001, there were 74 bookmobiles making over 700 school stops and over 2300 community stops in Ohio, circulating over 3,000,000 items.

Over time, bookmobile services ebbed according to the movement of the population, lessening as the suburbs built up. They still have a strong presence in rural areas, though. In 2000, the Geauga County Public Library was profiled by CNN.com for their bookmobile service to Amish country. Their bookmobile made fifty-two stops per week for the Amish alone. "The Amish do love us," said Pat Bonhard, one of the bookmobile staff, in the article. "When they see us, they smile. How many people in the service field can say that about their patrons?"

Rural areas are not the only places bookmobiles are used, however. The Columbus Metropolitan Library has MetroMouse Mobile Services. According to their website, it is designed to "put books in the hands of children." During the school year they target preschoolers and day-care centers, and during the summers, neighborhood stops. Library staff do storytimes for children, and teachers can check out "Wonderboxes" with books, flannel stories, and songs to use in their classrooms.

Services to seniors and to the homebound have also become an integral part of library services. Elizabeth Faries mentions this development in the April 1961 *Ohio Library Association Bulletin*: "services to shut-ins are a few of the new developments of recent years." Services targeting seniors began in 1946 with Cleveland Public Library's "Live Long and Like It" club. It was one of the first programs for seniors that addressed their mental and educational needs as well as their physical ones. Cleveland Public Library also ran workshops to train older volunteers to conduct children's story hours. According to a 1989 survey by Cuyahoga County Public Library, services to older adults reached their heyday in the mid-seventies, waning in the early eighties. Today, outreach departments continue to provide personalized service to the homebound. Martha Gardin, Director of the Greene County Public Library, has described outreach service as a "fairy-tale service." Books are delivered in person by the Greene County outreach staff, providing personalized reading materials and some much-needed company to the homebound. The library comes to them in a very real way.

Service to the homebound naturally extends to the hospitalized and the incarcerated. In 1846, the Ohio Penitentiary Library came into recognition, receiving its first aid from the state in 1854. In 1912, Cleveland Public Library opened an extensive hospital library, with a deposit and delivery station in a room of Cleveland State Hospital for the Insane. Notes from a 1977 conference, "Institution Library Perspectives," mentions library services in the Department of Rehabilitation and Corrections had expanded over $300,000 over the previous five-year period. Books in prison libraries, by necessity, range greatly, from elementary to college level, making building a collection a difficult endeavor. As of 1977, The Department of Corrections had hired six professional librarians over the past four years, and noted the Southern Ohio Correctional Facility as having the best prison library in the country. Libraries have continued to partner with correctional facilities to continue their mission: providing information to every Ohio resident, regardless of circumstance.

Serving those with disabilities has also been part of Ohio libraries' mission to have materials and resources for everyone in the state. Braille materials, especially, have been a focus of attention in Ohio, starting in 1900 when the Cincinnati Library Society for the Blind was established, with a librarian as president. Cleveland Public Library for the Blind was started with a small collection of books in 1903. In 1931, the Cincinnati Public Library and Cleveland Public Library were made regional distribution centers for free books for the blind. The Institution for the Deaf and Dumb was established in Columbus in 1951. Libraries today still provide services and accessibility for all patrons. One standard service is "talking books," which are specially recorded books from the Library for the Visually and Physically Handicapped.

As Ohio has developed, it has drawn large immigrant populations. Libraries have made a special effort to provide services to these groups, ranging from providing materials and programming in their native languages to providing English as a Second Language classes. Lorain Public Library has been particularly deliberate in providing services to their immigrant populations. In 1905, just a few years after the library started, Lorain Public owned forty books in German and fifteen in Hungarian. They also sponsored a program in March 1905 on Indians of the Northwest. Proceeds from admission went to "swell the library's German collection which is not adequate to the many demands of the readers." In 1907, Librarian Frances Root reported in her annual report that, "A relatively large proportion of the population of Lorain is foreign. The few books we have in Hungarian and German have been literally read to pieces. If we might have a gradually increasing collection of foreign books we should receive the active and most appreciative patronage of a new class of people." Two years later, they were circulating 1,355 foreign language books. By 1914, circulation of foreign books had nearly doubled to 2,515. In 1924, Lorain Public Library had 466 foreign language books. They continued to expand their foreign language collection throughout the twentieth century, including adding 500 Slovenian language books in 1952. Six years later, foreign language books included Hungarian, Italian, Russian, Ukrainian, Czech, German, and Slovenian. Spanish language books were added beginning in 1964.

In 1970, Lorain Public Library started a particularly exciting program, Project Libros, funded by LSCA. The money funded a Spanish-speaking field worker and additional Spanish language books. They also hired two bilingual staff to provide service to the Spanish-speaking community. The next year they were awarded a federal grant to continue Project Libros, and they added a Spanish-language film program. Project Libros continued through 1974, sponsoring a Hispanic Week Festival Cultural Hispano in 1973, drawing 1,300 people. The Project Libros field worker, Victor Torres, began a series of classes to prepare Spanish-speaking persons to pass the Spanish language version of the Ohio Driver's License examination, the first class of its kind. Libraries in Ohio have continued their service to immigrant populations today, including foreign language collections and English as a Second Language classes.

Libraries are now within the reach of every citizen of Ohio. Residents have not only embraced their local libraries; they've found ways to give back. The most obvious way of doing this is through the local Friends of the Library group. Friends groups have done everything from sponsoring book sales, with proceeds going to library needs, to working on building campaigns. *Friends Across Ohio*, a 1996 Ohio Library Council publication, describes Friends groups this way:

> The Friends are a volunteer support group. They look to the board and the director for guidance, inspiration, and leadership. The Friends give both tangible and intangible aid in the form of money, volunteer time, and expressions of support for library policies. What the Friends say and do does reflect on the library. The key word is support! If a group isn't behind the board's and director's goals and policies for the library, it isn't really a support group.

The history of Friends groups is a bit harder to trace. "Archival records of Friends groups usually do not exist or endure over time," according to Scott Bennett, as quoted in *The History of the Parma Heights Library*. Although their records have come and gone, Friends groups have been a backbone of support for innumerable Ohio libraries.

Ohio libraries have been trendsetting in their programming for communities at large. Ohio's population has changed radically in its two-hundred-plus years. Ohio started as a wilderness, populated by plucky pioneers determined to carve out a life for themselves. As Ohio has grown and changed, so have Ohio libraries. Ohio's libraries have reached out to the homebound, the disabled, the illiterate, and the non-English speaking. Ohio's libraries have not been bound by their walls. They have had a collective vision of reaching the entire population of Ohio, and through outreach and other services, they have. What started as a rather exclusive subscription service has grown into a public library service accessible to every resident of Ohio. Public libraries exist because of the patronage and support of Ohio's residents, and their determination to make information accessible to all.

Library Trustees
David C. Miller

More than 1,600 trustees link Ohio's 250 public library districts to their communities through their dual roles of being stewards of taxpayer dollars and advocates for the library patrons of today and tomorrow. Trustees are responsible for the spending of state funds, ranging from as little as $55,000 annually in Alger to $52 million per year in Cincinnati. Many public libraries also have local tax levies to supplement the state funding that historically places Ohio's libraries among the highest in the nation in per capita state funding.

Trustees must also reflect their communities in determining what library services the residents need. Representing a diverse assortment of professions, including information technology, trustees also fill a variety of niches—from the parents of pre-school children to those representing fellow senior citizens. Many trustees are former employees of both public and school libraries. Some trustees may represent specific geographic areas in a library district, while others are on library boards simply because of their love for libraries.

Although they share the bond of appreciating the many roles libraries fill in any community, trustees can find themselves on different sides of the philosophical fence regarding issues such as consolidation of library districts and intellectual freedom when it's applied to Internet access by library patrons of all ages. Trustees often become extremely protective of their libraries' funding base and the perceived growing threat of that funding being at the political mercy of state legislators.

Some trustees believe the greatest strength of Ohio's library community is the fact that there are 250 library districts reflecting the uniqueness of their communities. Other trustees believe that fewer districts would result in more political clout at the statehouse, and many advocate for only eighty-eight districts—one for each county.

Roles of Trustees

In connecting their communities to their libraries, trustees represent two distinct constituencies: taxpayers and library patrons. A trustee must have his or her "finger on the pulse of the community," according to Lucille Hastings, a former trustee of the Holmes County District Public Library. The trustee should have "an idea of what the community is interested in" getting from the library. For instance, in Holmes County, "We couldn't be without a bookmobile here. We have a lot of stops that we make for the Amish."

"When we've had some difficulties" with the public being at odds with the library, she said the board included "some people who were not understanding what the community wanted." One of those times involved the way the board announced plans to close two of the library's branches. "People were very upset. The public took them over." One group started over with the same building. "They elected local people from the community and they still have story hours and events." A second group of citizens tried to do the same thing with the other building, but Hastings said, "They felt they were an after-school babysitting service, and that is now where the historical society keeps its records."

Planned closings of branches generated similar problems for the board of the Cincinnati Public Library. Long-time Cincinnati trustee Charlie Lindberg explained that "last summer [2002] the director recommended that we close six of our branch libraries" to adjust the budget to a freeze in state funding. "When we said we would follow that recommendation, there was an eruption in the communities about the closing of their libraries." After the board held a series of public hearings on the issue, it decided not to close any branches. Instead, Lindberg said, the board cut its budget by reducing the hours of operation for all libraries in the system. "The board has to keep its ears to the ground to make certain we don't get too far afield from the wishes of the public," Lindberg said.

Jim Switzer, a former president of the Ohio Library Trustees Association and a nine-year member trustee of the Akron-Summit County Public Library, said his job as a trustee "is to make the librarian's job doable." Terry Casey, who served two seven-year terms on the Columbus Metropolitan Library board, admits that "Most people have no idea who's really in charge and what really happens in running libraries. People are busy in their daily lives and don't have the time or interests to worry about such issues."

Joan Loeffler was president of the Ida Rupp Public Library Board in Port Clinton for thirty of the thirty-six years she served as a trustee. Trustees, she said, "can bring knowledge of the community" to help direct the library. Their focus, she said, is in the service provided by the library, whether that involves community room usage or service to any minorities. "We could disagree—if you knew that their aim was better service to the community. You just have to decide what it is."

In addition to setting library policies, another key responsibility of a board "is selecting the right person to run the library," said Loeffler. Mary Obenour, a former trustee of the Muskingum County Library System, was honored in 1993 as the Ohio Trustee of the Year. She believes trustees should "represent the general public—the community—to the library, and the library to the community." The major job of trustees, she said, "is to watch the money. Fiscal responsibility certainly rests with the trustee. The trustee does not interfere with the running of the library. The director is responsible for the day-to-day operations."

Relationship between the Board and the Director

While most trustees find common ground when discussing perceptions of their role, they travel some different paths when it comes to what they feel should be the relationships between trustees and their library directors. Some avoid becoming close friends with their directors, while others see no problem with such friendships.

"No surprises" appears to be a common theme that trustees want in their relationship with directors. "There should be a good give and take—not confrontational," Hastings said. "They should come to a consensus of some sort." Trustees, she added, "can't go in with an agenda of their own." To make the correct decisions, "the board needs to be willing to be educated." Hastings believes that the friendship between trustees and directors should not be too cozy. She also explained that she "tried not to have too many private meetings with the director. Everybody needed to be included" in discussions of interest to the board.

Switzer said his library director "keeps the board well apprised" on topics such as budget development. "We do a lot of talking, but it's not board-driven. We have a very good CPA board member, a widely experienced board member, who starts asking real questions" when the director comes to them with recommendations. When the library recently built fifteen new branches and doubled the size of the main facility, the board relied on its director to chart the course.

Casey sees more of a need for directors to rely on the expertise of trustees. "The good news is that great library leaders, and there are many, see the bigger picture and value trustees for many roles. But most of the mass of librarians are more narrowly focused and missing the trendline for how fast the information world is changing! Good trustees can really help great librarians manage those changes. I don't think they have a course at the MLS level to teach directors how to work with, manage, and get the most out of trustees and community leaders. But knowing how to use trustees for those positive purposes can play a major role in making your library the best.

"Good directors want, need, and value good trustees. Some directors are frustrated by trustees who are not up-to-date on the issues of the day for libraries—technology, etc. Good directors get lots out of quality trustees. But a certain number of directors like to treat trustees like mushrooms … keep them in the dark and feed them [manure]."

Loeffler brought up a fairly prevalent criticism directed toward boards of trustees in decades gone by—they had a history of not paying competitive wages to librarians. "They were not miserly, but frugal," she said, putting as positive of a spin on it as anyone could. "Today," she noted, "everybody's consciousness has been raised" from the time when boards might say when hiring a new director, "Her husband has a good job, so we don't have to pay her much."

"I see it working more as a partnership between trustees and the director and the clerk, and they all work together," Moore said. "We are able to do our part of the job and help the director with hers." "Vital to a good partnership," she said, "is open communication."

The key to the trustee-director relationship for Jo Homyak, who served twenty-three years on the Huron Library board, is "listening to each other, respecting others opinions. We work together to come to a consensus. You're not interfering with the decisions of that person. You're not going down to the library and saying 'why don't you do this?' If you see things you think should be changed, you talk with the director or bring it up at a meeting."

Trustees are involved in "setting policy, making decisions such as whether we should expand. You leave the day-to-day decisions to the director. The board has to be very careful not to micro-manage," Lindberg said, adding, "At the same time, there are some political issues that the board might be more attuned to than [the] staff or the director."

Filling Vacancies on Boards

More than 150 of Ohio's 250 library districts are school district libraries, with the seven trustees on each board being appointed by their boards of education. Another fifty-plus are county district libraries, with county commissioners appointing four of the trustees and the common pleas judges appointing the other three.

The other types of library districts are municipal, with the mayor appointing the six trustees; association, with the charters of the associations spelling out how trustees are appointed and the number of trustees on each board varying according to their charters; township, with township trustees appointing the three trustees on each of these four boards; and county (not the same as county district), with common pleas judges appointing the six trustees on each of the three county boards. Most library boards have some opportunity for input into the appointment process. Not ironically, perhaps, the opportunity for input is usually greatest in the smaller districts and very limited on the metropolitan boards, where the appointments are generally more political.

"When we suggested a couple names, we were told we may not do that—that it's none of our business," said Switzer. "They give us people who don't show up; they said it only takes an hour a month. ... We're in the middle of a building project. Committee work is extremely important," he said. "Once we get the buildings built, we can go back to being a sleepy board."

Even Cincinnati's board doesn't play a major role in filling its vacancies, said Lindberg, a trustee since 1982. "I got involved because I had spent five years on the Cincinnati Board of Education, serving as president for two years." His appointment to the library board "flowed from that." Vacancies on library boards are "semi-political," he said, with the appointments by the county commissioners and judges.

But in small library districts such as Alger, Moore added, the board is active in helping to fill vacancies. "We're a school district library. We submit a nomination to them [the school board]." The nominating committee meets in November to survey "a pool of many people from all areas of the district, with a wide range of different backgrounds" to see who among them might meet the needs of the board. The Alger board currently includes a retired schoolteacher, school librarian, and human resources professional, explained Moore, who fills another niche as a full-time mother with a two-year-old and a newborn.

Trustees "should be willing to give whatever time it takes" to get the job done, according to Hastings. Some people "just like to be appointed to boards; they don't understand the work involved. We look for someone who's dedicated and willing to live up to their responsibility on the board."

The Holmes library board has attempted to have some geographic representation—an approach strongly supported by the judges and commissioners. "We try to get good information about different segments of the community. We've always tried to have a mix of men and women. A lot are just ordinary working people. We need to have someone [who is] just a 'regular Joe worker-type' person; it gives you that variety of perspectives."

In Port Clinton, Loeffler said, the school board permits the library board to make a recommendation. The criteria used in selecting a member, she said, are fairly straightforward: "You have to choose somebody that is respected in community, who has served on a volunteer board, completed a project, and demonstrates their willingness to do the work."

Obenour said, "We are extremely fortunate in Muskingum County that our library trustees are not political trustees. I think it's a tragedy when that happens." Political appointees often have "an ax to grind or they're looking for a line on their job resume," added Obenour, who served on the board for twenty-one years, starting in 1978. Whether the appointment will be made by the commissioners or the judge, she said, "We recommend two names and they are very supportive. We try to get people with expertise, such as investment people, building contractors, attorneys—as well as 'plain ordinary citizens' who use our library." In Huron, Homyak said, the trustees used to give the school board a list of people interested in being on the board. "The superintendent then decided we should only submit one name. I think that was an error. It gives you a potential situation where you only put someone on there who feels like we feel.

"I believe in diversity on the board. It should not be all professionals or college grads. It should be a mixture of people," including one or two people whose special interest is "just" being a library patron. Homyak feels that "It's great to have someone who uses the library. There are a lot of obituary boards."

Library Funding

Since January 1, 1986, Ohio's public libraries have received state funding through the Library and Local Government Support Fund (LLGSF). From 1931 through 1985, they were supported by the intangibles tax. The original LLGSF formula provided libraries with 6.3 percent of the personal income tax collections. That percentage was reduced to 5.7 percent in 1995.

At the start of the budget process for the 2004–5 biennium, with Ohio facing severe cuts in state funding of all services, some members of the Ohio House of Representatives were considering eliminating the LLGSF. That would have a catastrophic impact on Ohio libraries, which collectively received $496 million in LLGSF funds during 2001, before sliding to $458 million in 2002. Switching to the LLGSF in the 1980s "was a huge change," according to Hastings. "The reporting of the intangibles was not done very well; a lot of people were not reporting it. I don't know how much the Amish reported, for instance. When they went to the new formula the money went up by huge amounts. It has provided a lot of opportunities"—from "buying books that we never had before" to being able to pay for a new building.

"We knew we needed to have a better facility. But we didn't see how we could ask for a levy. So we started stashing money away (from the additional LLGSF monies). We were also able to get some federal money for a building program and then we finally were able to build a new library." Since then, she added, "Circulation just mushroomed at the new library in Millersburg." But Hastings admits that "I was always worried because I felt we were operating at the pleasure of the legislature" that could control the LLGSF purse strings.

For both the Columbus library and Ohio libraries in general, Casey said, "Money makes a big, big difference. Ohio would not be number one right now, nor even close," had it not been for the switch to LLGSF funding. "Both the dollars themselves, plus the better ability to do long-range planning, have made a huge difference.

"And the big growth of money came at the right time to deal with the increasing hunger for information, plus all of the technology/ Internet change. The late 1990s was a huge run-up period in funding and it matched the period of most need. And do not forget the huge advantage that Ohio has in governance. Libraries are not a part of city or county government. Directors don't have to compete with police, fire, and garbage for dollars and city manager/mayor attentions. Compared to most parts of America, that governance factor is really big."

Cincinnati's library system "did very well under intangibles," said Lindberg. "We never had to worry about political folks changing the percentages or freezing them." With Cincinnati "being one of few big libraries that have no local property tax" to supplement the state's funds, he said, "we worry every year about what the legislature is going to do" with the LLGSF formula. During 2001, Cincinnati received more than $52 million from the LLGSF. There always have been some "pressures from the legislature or other interest groups, but not to the extent there is now," he added.

Increased funding through LLGSF has allowed the Ida Rupp Public Library to hire not only more, but better educated staff members, Loeffler said. "We have two people with MLS degrees on our staff now." The library currently has twenty-two employees and is able to "pay for some tuition" costs for them to get more education.

In Zanesville, Obenour said, there "wasn't any money from the intangibles tax." She added that "we had a few board members who were a little bit tight" with what few dollars there were. "So we went through a couple of stages where things were pretty rocky." Because of tight budgeting, "There was a time when it was hard for us to get a director. When the funding changed in the mid eighties, we went for a bond issue, which barely passed." The board was then able to "put in some new branches."

Consolidation

Public library trustees in Ohio are intensely proud of their own libraries. Many trustees will say they have the best library among libraries "our size" in the state. So these trustees don't take kindly to even the whisper of the word "consolidation." Merging their libraries with adjacent ones is usually seen as not only watering down a good thing, but as losing local control. They regard the fact that Ohio has 250 independent library boards as a very important strength of Ohio's public library system.

However, many directors and trustees of Ohio's larger libraries believe that the large number is a detriment to efficiency and also an irritant to the Ohio General Assembly. They often say that General Assembly committee members express the hope that Ohio will someday have fewer library districts. One representative of a large library said, "They're nice folks and have good people on the board. But if they became a branch of us they would have more money and a better library. And I'll bet there are fifties libraries in the same situation."

But most members of the General Assembly are also aware of the political wars that would be fought against consolidation by the trustees and directors of libraries in their own districts. Because of this potential, consolidation "is a word you never mention," said Jim Switzer of the Akron Public Library Board. "I still shake my head at the idea of 250 library districts" in one state, he admitted. But, he added, "the time for the *c-word* may be coming," referring to the tightening of the state funding for libraries.

Hastings has been a member of her local library board, her regional library board, and the State Library of Ohio Board. She's well aware of the efficiencies that come through "group buying, use of shared consultants, such as technology experts. You have that in the regionals—where a technology person would help all the libraries; they couldn't afford to have their own technology experts." However, she's a firm believer that "there has to be somebody making decisions at the local level. There's just something useful in having your own library—having it tailored more to your line of thinking. We have a different drumbeat than other people have. People would resent having administration from some metropolitan area. That's a hard thing to overcome. You work at the approval, the appreciation, of the community." Hastings added that, "It isn't that the community isn't willing to change, but it needs to be initiated locally."

Alger Public Library's Moore agreed with Hastings. "I do like the idea that each of the libraries has its own board," she said. Having that many library districts allows them to be "tailor-made to their area—making this something that fits the needs of this area very well. We try harder," Moore sincerely believes. "We're a little treasure in our county—maybe its best-kept secret." If her library merged with another, she said, the new board "wouldn't really know what this area really needs."

Future Challenges

As Ohio celebrates its bicentennial year, public library trustees face increasing challenges. State budget problems threaten Ohio's status as being one of the top states in state per capita funding for libraries. The rapidly changing world of technology is both a positive and a negative for public libraries. It puts some of the greatest databases at the literal fingertips of even the smallest of Ohio's libraries. But technology is also a financial drain in terms of hardware, software, and skilled human resources. The days are long gone when trustees only had to focus on the budget line items of material acquisitions and personnel.

But the more things change, the more they remain the same for library trustees. The primary challenge trustees face is determining how their libraries fit into a society that seems to be getting busier each year—a situation probably similar to that encountered at the dawn of the early days of radio and later television. Library trustees have the never-ending task of making their libraries relevant to their communities, responding to the needs of the hour while being as fiscally accountable as humanly possible.

Each trustee brings his or her own unique perspective to the board table. Collectively they provide a wealth of expertise in helping to guide their libraries into Ohio's third century. Regardless of the year, the goal of library trustees, as stated by Cincinnati's Lindberg, "is to preserve and to enhance the services of the public library so that we are offering the citizens a library system second to none."

Intellectual Freedom

JEFF FRENCH and CINDY LOMBARDO

What Is Intellectual Freedom?

Every library in the country should have a sign on the door reading: THIS LIBRARY HAS SOMETHING OFFENSIVE TO EVERYONE. IF YOU ARE NOT OFFENDED BY SOMETHING WE OWN, PLEASE COMPLAIN.
—Dorothy Broderick, American Libraries (May, 1993)

INTELLECTUAL FREEDOM—THE RIGHT OF EVERY INDIVIDUAL to seek and receive information and opinions from all points of view—has become a hallmark of Ohio libraries, ranked number one among libraries across the nation in terms of funding and service. From the beginning, the relationship between Ohio's public libraries and intellectual freedom has been consistently complex and frequently contentious, as it has been for the nation. As the leading professional organization for librarians in the United States, the American Library Association intentionally never has endorsed a specific definition of the term "intellectual freedom," but rather has focused on crafting a set of principles that foster a climate of unrestricted access to information. This lack of a specific definition is in keeping with the ALA's longstanding contention that public libraries are best governed locally rather than being forced to subscribe to a one-size-fits-all set of regulations.

The stance of librarians toward intellectual freedom, and all that it implies, varies widely, and examples can be found within all states of public librarians who hold vastly divergent views on issues ranging from what minors should and should not be able to read, view, and hear, to the types of magazines that are "appropriate" for the library's collection, and the use of filters in restricting access to certain websites. Certainly, with the advent of the Internet, the magnitude of this divergence has dramatically increased and has led to passionate, sometimes strident, and not always civilized, debate within the library community. With each new format (paperback series, video, CD, DVD, Internet) the debate begins anew as to the role that libraries, and librarians, can and should play in information access.

How Has Intellectual Freedom Evolved?

The roles that public librarians play today are dramatically different than they were up through the early 1900s. Initially, librarians (at that time almost exclusively male) were expected to serve as arbiters of public decency and culture, and a major part of their work involved selecting works of literature they believed were worthy of inclusion in their collections. Perhaps not surprisingly, the definition of what was worthy tended to be fairly narrowly constrained and to embrace only those ideas and opinions that upheld the traditional values of the upper economic class. The notion of a popular reading collection was unknown; rather, the emphasis was on reading and appreciating the classics and other printed works that were promulgated to ennoble, uplift, and inspire, rather than entertain or inform.

However, as with other cultural institutions, libraries were forced to respond to the changing social and political tenor of their times. The flood of immigrants to American shores, the rise of industry, and the creation of the middle and lower middle classes created an overwhelming need for widespread and low-cost public education. Libraries responded by becoming centers of "education for the masses" rather than retreats for the elite. Yet the emphasis on traditional values and norms remained. However, as the country grew and prospered, libraries began to change to encompass a more democratic and diverse populace. Today, we see the epitome of this evolution to a information democracy in Cleveland Public Library's slogan—THE PEOPLES' UNIVERSITY.

Prior to the 1930s, the American Library Association played only a minimal role in challenging attempted censorship of library materials. It was not until 1939, when John Steinbeck's *The Grapes of Wrath* became the target of censorship attempts because of the social views advanced by the author and the accused "immorality" of the book's content that the ALA adopted The Library's Bill of Rights (the precursor to the present Library Bill of Rights, which was adopted in 1948), a pivotal document dealing with intellectual freedom principles. One year later, the ALA established the Intellectual Freedom Committee with the charge to "recommend such steps as may be necessary to safeguard the rights of library users in accordance with the Bill of Rights and the Library's Bill of Rights ..." These actions were taken at a time when much of Europe was sealed behind the Iron Curtain and citizens in these countries were severely punished for open political speech. Since then, librarians nationwide have turned for help to the American Library Association when facing censorship challenges, whether they be on religious, sexual, political, or social ground.

The *Library Bill of Rights* is grounded firmly in the First Amendment to the United States Constitution (ratified December 15, 1791), which states "Congress shall make no law respecting an establishment of religion, or prohibiting the free exercise thereof; or abridging the freedom of speech, or of the press; or the right of the people peaceably to assemble; and to petition the Government for a redress of grievances." Its overriding concept is that democracy requires free and open access to information in order to produce informed citizens capable of making effective self-governance decisions.

Over the years, the *Library Bill of Rights* has undergone numerous amendments and revisions. According to the *Intellectual Freedom Manual* (6th edition), the original document focused on unbiased book selection, the importance of a balanced collection, and the provision of open meeting rooms. Later additions to the document addressed directive removal of materials (i.e., the deletion or excision of parts of published materials as well as efforts to ban, prohibit, suppress, proscribe, remove, label, or restrict materials), opposition to the censorship of non-print media, exclusion of materials because of the social views of the authors, and the importance of respecting the protection of library materials afforded by the First Amendment. Many public library boards of trustees have adopted the *Library Bill of Rights* and have included it in the policy manuals of their respective libraries. As new information formats evolve, they bring with them new questions relative to intellectual freedom and necessitate review of the Library Bill of Rights, frequently resulting in the development of position statements that clarify how the document should be applied. The most recent example is "Access to Electronic Information, Services, and Networks: an Interpretation of the Library Bill of Rights" (adopted by the ALA Council, January 24, 1996).

Why Does It Matter?

Within the past decade, certainly nothing has created more controversy for public libraries than the advent of the Internet and the benefits and problems inherent in providing public access to this electronic medium. This has been particularly true in Ohio because of the Ohio Public Library Information Network (OPLIN)—a state-funded program that provided funding for Internet access to all 250 public libraries across the state. In July of 1997, the Supreme Court struck down the Communications Decency Act (CDA), affirming in a 9–0 decision that communications over the Internet deserve the highest level of constitutional protection (American Library Association v. U.S. Department of Justice and Reno v. American Civil Liberties Union). The Court stated that Internet communications warrant the same level of first amendment protection as books, magazines, newspapers, and speakers on a street-corner soapbox. In essence, this decision guaranteed Americans the same access to information in cyberspace as what they have on library and bookstore shelves. As part of their participation in OPLIN, every Ohio library has adopted an acceptable use policy that spells out in detail local, board-developed guidelines for Internet and computer use within the library.

The Internet embodies an exponentially escalating wealth of data, much of it unorganized and all of it (unless restricted by some type of filter) accessible to library customers who often have little knowledge of effective searching techniques and minimal skills in evaluating the accuracy, timeliness, and potential bias of the information they call forth on the computer screen. The Internet exemplifies a medium that offers all points of view, from the religious right to the liberal left and everywhere in between, and provides material on every nuance of every topic imaginable.

Today's librarians are struggling with a plethora of intellectual freedom issues and questions, not all of which involve the Internet. Challenges to print and audiovisual materials continue with regularity. Some raise their voices in protest against children's books that portray nontraditional families in a positive way. Others protest children's books like *Huckleberry Finn* that they deem "politically incorrect," "racist," or "stereotyping." Still others object to the wildly popular Harry Potter series by English author J.K. Rowling on the grounds that they promote witchcraft and Satanism. "Request for Reconsideration of Materials" forms continue to cross the desks of library directors citing customers' objections to sexual content, inappropriate language, anti-religious themes, and anti-family values. Yet perhaps it is this very receptivity and invitation to criticism from, and dialogue with, their customers on the part of librarians that make today's libraries so much more robust than those from the early 1900s and identify them as uniquely democratic institutions.

Who Censors and Why

Studies by the Freedom Forum repeatedly have shown that although Americans value their freedom of speech more than the other freedoms guaranteed by the Bill of Rights, they often are also willing to restrict that freedom. When speech gets uncomfortable, a common reaction is the desire to avoid it; from that desire comes the urge to censor library collections. Librarians try to remember that would-be censors usually come with good intentions. The censors' desire to protect someone, often children, from ideas that are offensive, harmful, or threatening, is often sincere, but just as often due to a misunderstanding of the role of libraries in providing access to, rather than promotion of, ideas and information. In a censorship challenge, libraries frequently find themselves in the middle between competing public interests—the desire to protect and the American value of freedom of speech.

The Amherst Public Library and the Medina County District Library both faced challenges that eventually coincided with levy campaigns. Amherst's started with an objection to the videotape *The Last Temptation of Christ* due to its offensiveness to some Christians. In Medina, a variety of complaints ultimately led to objections to minors' Internet access and a very public debate over the library's policies. Tax levies in both cases became a focus of the challenges with opponents seeing the defeat of the levy as a way to pressure the library into abandoning its policy; however, voters in both communities passed the libraries' tax initiatives, effectively underscoring the communities' support of their First Amendment rights to the information offered by the library. Just as the Freedom Forum survey found, American citizens value freedom of speech highly.

A protest doesn't have to reach the point of a formal challenge to library policies, practices, and collections for the library to find itself in the middle of a conflict. The experience of the Cleveland Heights–University Heights Public Library (CH–UH) with Madonna's book, *Sex*, is a perfect illustration of the difficulties a library may face in providing popular material that some in the community find offensive.

Madonna's book was a cultural event. The author's popularity, combined with the controversial nature of her book of erotic writings and pictures, guaranteed interest. A lot of libraries shied away from purchasing her book, which provided several ready-made excuses for any internal censorship librarians wanted to practice. At $50, it was expensive for its time. It came in a spiral binding with a metal cover. Reviews, while indicating its probable popularity, criticized the quality of its writing and photography. Many librarians, worried by the potential for conflict over the book's content, readily accepted any excuse not to buy it. Spiral bindings were held to be flimsy, difficult to label and therefore, hard to shelve accurately. The metal cover was said to interfere with magnetic security gates. The reviews were poor; the writing was bad; the photography was grainy and poorly reproduced. And on and on, despite the popularity of spiral bound cookbooks, the falsity of the security gate story, and the common availability in libraries of numerous other poorly written and poorly illustrated works. Even libraries whose selection policies specified the purchase of books on the *New York Times* bestseller list shied away from *Sex* because of its controversial nature.

Seeing the popularity of the book, and following a policy of using popularity, as well as quality, as a selection criterion, CH–UH purchased the book. With a reserve list in the mid-seventies and a desired reserve to copy ratio of 5:1, the library wanted to buy about fifteen copies. However, after exhausting its jobbers and local bookstores, the library learned that it could provide only eight copies. As a result, the library found itself in the middle of a minor controversy. Criticized on one hand for having purchased more copies per capita than any other public library in Ohio, the library also had to field complaints from customers who pointed out that the waiting list was too long and wanted the library to buy more. Despite the controversial nature of the book, the library did its best to guarantee access to it for those in the community who were interested. Having been criticized on both sides for this selection decision, the staff felt that if everyone was angry with them they must have found a truly well balanced position.

How each library fashions policies to fit its local community is of crucial importance. CH–UH, with a community considered very open minded, insisted on and was supported in providing access to ideas and information the residents wanted, and expected any who were offended by something to exercise their right to choose not to read it. Despite a large Jewish community, this library was able to provide anti-Semitic writings, such as *Hoax of the Twentieth Century*, in the spirit of exploring all sides of an issue, and was able to do so without challenges. Other library boards, exercising their local control, could fashion their policies according to their local needs. The Columbus Metropolitan Library's policy specified that the library would purchase no pornography. When the popular author Anne Rice stated in an interview that her earlier pseudonymous writings as A.N. Roquelaure were pornographic, the library had no choice but to remove these books from their collection.

Often new formats engender new challenges. When libraries were in the dying stages of trying to provide a prescriptive, uplifting collection, it was common to question the quality of paperback books. Libraries were slow to adopt this format and this reluctance is still seen in the lingering practice of not fully cataloguing paperbacks, as if their role in the collection is less important than that of hardbound books. Libraries were slow to include rock-and-roll music in their collections, and even slower to catalogue it, seeing it first as a passing fad with no lasting value, an interpretation belied by the creation of the Rock Hall of Fame in Cleveland.

Sometimes the change from printed to visual images spurs challenges. Libraries' philosophical desire to treat videotapes with the same policies that govern books has led to numerous problems. Akron Summit County Public Library endured a challenge regarding their videotape policies that eventually led to their restricting minors' access to the collection, but other libraries willingly imposed similar restrictions. As in the case of Madonna, reasons were sometimes ephemeral, for example, citing the cost of videotapes, parents' unwillingness to assume financial responsibility for their children's movies, and confusing the rating system developed by the MPAA with a legal restriction on what libraries may purchase or what minors may borrow. Some libraries backed out of buying popular titles, claiming an unwillingness to compete with video rental stores and focusing on documentary, classic, and foreign films. Other libraries, though, treated videotapes with the same free-access policies as the rest of their collection, insisted on parents' responsibility to regulate their own children, and provided the variety of popular movies their communities desired. The resulting boom in circulation testifies to their communities' demand for these materials.

The Internet is the most recent instance of a new format threatening traditional controls and stirring community interest in restricting access. With the Internet's lack of central, controlling authority, the role of publishers is diminished. Quality control is nonexistent and the range of ideas expressed is unlimited. With the lack of control over what is available, the general public, parents, and politicians hope to reestablish their control over the more troubling side of the Internet. Even librarians often are uncomfortable with the Internet because once a library provides Internet access; the staff loses control over what comes into the library as a result of that access. The librarian's role as *selector* is diminished as customers may now choose to view any Internet information they desire.

The desire to control an essentially uncontrollable entity has led to attempted legislation at both the federal and state level. Congress has tried repeatedly to exert some control over the Internet by passing a variety of laws, such as the Communications Decency Act (CDA), the Children's Online Protection Act (COPA), and the Children's Internet Protection Act (CIPA). All were found to run afoul of the United States Constitution in the Federal Courts. The Supreme Court found the CDA unconstitutional and COPA and CIPA have been found unconstitutional by district courts. COPA has been returned to the District Court level for reconsideration and the Supreme Court will hear arguments concerning the constitutionality of CIPA in 2003.

State government attempts to limit free speech are exemplified by the passage of House Bill 8, the Ohio legislature's attempt to expand the Harmful to Minors law to the Internet. Even though the Harmful to Minors act is not limited by format, the General Assembly still passed this law in an attempt to control Internet content analogous to the Federal government's CDA, COPA and CIPA efforts. In 2002, a coalition of opponents filed suit in US District Court to challenge the constitutionality of HB8.

Current events often exert an influence and urge toward censorship. For example, just as the terrorist attacks of September 11, 2002, led directly to passage of the USA PATRIOT Act, which allows the Federal Government to access previously confidential patron records and Internet searches, and thus compromising library patrons' rights to read and research freely, smaller events will exert pressure to restrict access to "offensive" material. Reports of child abuse facilitated by Internet communications result in attempts to restrict Internet content or access. The release of a popular, but controversial movie, such as *The Last Temptation of Christ*, or of a popular, controversial book, such as Madonna's *Sex* or *The Satanic Verses* by Salman Rushdie, almost inevitably results in complaints about similar materials in libraries. After the Columbine shootings, many parents became more concerned with their children's activities, and the ability to monitor those activities resulted in legislation affecting Ohio's libraries in the form of a new confidentiality law.

Ohio libraries' defense of patron confidentiality has been mixed. Without any law protecting the confidentiality of patron records, Ohio's libraries for years relied on their own local confidentiality policies. Typically, a library held that records of patrons' transactions were confidential and would be shared only with the patron whose records were in question. However, the issue of whether or not these records were subject to the Public Records provisions was in doubt until 1999 when the General Assembly finally gave patron records protection from public scrutiny.

A confidentiality law resulted from a controversy regarding parents' access to their children's records. A man in Greene County wanting to know what his child had charged out from the library asked to see those records. The library, whose policy kept all records confidential, refused to provide them. The man appealed to his local legislator, Representative Steve Austria, who planned to introduce a bill forcing libraries to release children's records to their parents. The Ohio Library Council successfully lobbied Rep. Austria for some confidentiality protection. The result, House Bill 389, requires that a library keep confidential records related to a patron's transactions with the library as well as any personal information on its patrons. In effect, any records a library keeps on a patron and any information connecting a patron's name with any titles, subjects, or reference requests that patron has used or made, are to be kept private between the library and the patron.

There are a few exceptions, which provide for access with a court order or search warrant, for patrons who want to give others access to their records, and for library administrative purposes, but the most controversial exception relates to minors' records. As was Representative Austria's original intent, the bill provides that a library must release the records of a minor child to that child's parents, guardian, or custodian. This provision presents several procedural problems for libraries, the most difficult being the identification of a child's true parents. It makes no distinction between custodial and non-custodial parents, and is unclear regarding the applicability to children of the waiver of confidentiality provision. Its biggest flaw, though, is in its denial of Ohio's minors' privacy. Librarians are concerned that there may well be occasions in which release of a minor's library records to parents could be harmful. For example, a child looking for information on relief from an abusive family, or a teen exploring alternate lifestyles in a family hostile to that idea is ill served if the library must release this information to a violent parent. Divorced parents with a history of violence could use the parental provision to locate their children and abduct or otherwise harm them.

While libraries celebrate the fact that adults' records are now confidential, and that minors' records are confidential from everyone except their parents, guardians, and custodians, the parental exception in HB389 makes many librarians nervous. Ohio's libraries, which have traditionally supported everyone's right to desired information, are dismayed by the General Assembly's stronger support for adults' rights than for the rights of minors. Given the usual government intent to protect children from harm, this exception is a curious oversight.

How Librarians Respond

Ohio's libraries have several methods at their disposal in their quest to protect citizens' rights to read, view, and listen to the ideas, information, and entertainment they choose. Foremost among these methods is the authority of local library boards to establish library policy. Each library board has the authority and responsibility to set policy that will help meet the needs of its community. In the interest of protecting the community's right to information, most library boards endorse the recommended Intellectual Freedom policies of the American Library Association, including the *Library Bill of Rights*, its interpretations, the *Librarian's Code of Ethics*, and the "Libraries: an American Value" statement. These ALA-recommended policies serve as the foundation for each library's collection development and service policies and guarantee a balanced collection and free access to library services for all.

Support of these policies is so strong that it is not uncommon for libraries to insist that their staff understand them and be prepared to enforce them vigilantly. Many libraries include discussion of

Intellectual Freedom issues in their employment interviews to assure that new staff members understand these principles and are willing to support the library's policies. These concepts are part of many libraries' orientation and training and also may be included in the continuing education and development of staff. When faced with a problem or challenge, libraries can seek assistance from a number of sources. The American Library Association's Office on Intellectual Freedom is a prime resource of sample documents, legal advice, and other support.

Ohio is also extremely fortunate to have an active Intellectual Freedom Committee. Under the auspices of the Ohio Library Council, this committee can help with challenges and lend guidance and advice to libraries making policy decisions. The committee provides an educational program on intellectual freedom called "Meeting the Challenge," that can be presented at staff development day, staff meetings, and board meetings. The program discusses the principle of intellectual freedom, its role in library policy and procedure, and provides guidance in evaluating a library's practices for complying with the ideals of free speech and free access. Thanks to the efforts of committee volunteers, this program is available free to any library in Ohio and has been presented throughout the state for more than a decade. The committee's work on this program was recognized nationally when it won the SIRS State and Regional Achievement Award at the 2000 ALA Annual Conference in Chicago.

Cooperation with other organizations that support freedom of speech and oppose censorship is vital to the efforts of Ohio's libraries. The library community has had particular success in cooperative ventures with the Ohio Educational Library and Media Association (OELMA) and with the American Civil Liberties Union Ohio (ACLU). OELMA and OLC sponsored a statewide conference on Intellectual Freedom in 1994 and formerly cosponsored a concurrent annual conference. The ACLU has helped with educational programs presented at OLC annual and chapter conferences, and recognized the Intellectual Freedom Committee with their 2001 Liberty's Flame Award for work in support of civil liberties. Individual libraries offer community education regarding their role in a free society and also build partnerships with local organizations, developing an alliance of friends who understand the library's role and support it in times of conflict.

A final part in libraries' protection of their community's free access to information is in the form of lobbying. Ohio's libraries, through the Ohio Library Council, actively lobby the General Assembly for favorable legislation. Examples of these lobbying efforts include a drive for confidentiality legislation and opposition to government-imposed Internet filtering.

Conclusion

Ohio's libraries take very seriously their role in protecting the state's residents' right to information. The strongest tool at the library's disposal is the system of local control in place through the representation of the community on the library's board of trustees. Trustees are entrusted with the protection of and respect for the individual library customer's freedom of choice. It is the trustees who decide the policies for each library that are appropriate for their community. They are the body that guarantees the community's access to ideas and information; the community's right to read, view and listen to the materials they select; the community's ability to find the information they need to make decisions, to participate in the political process, and to vote intelligently. In this role, the trustees and their libraries embody the essence of democracy: facilitating the community's ability to exercise its freedom and govern itself.

Defending the Right to Information: A Case Study
—Jeff French

At times, the library is the community's first line of defense of the freedom to information. In May 1997, the Ohio General Assembly considered attaching a requirement to filter libraries' Internet access to the bill providing funding for the Ohio Public Library Information Network (OPLIN). James Kuhn, a librarian at the University of Akron and chair of the Ohio Library Council's Intellectual Freedom Committee presented testimony before the Ohio Senate's Finance and Financial Institutions Committee opposing the mandating of filters in Ohio's libraries. Kuhn pointed out that the ALA Library Bill of Rights was adopted in 1948, when much of Europe was behind the Iron Curtain and many countries punished self-expression. Librarians created this document in an attempt to guarantee free access to information with the intent of helping preserve self-government through an informed electorate. Pointing out that filters would limit access to information for those who rely on the library as their only point of entry to the Internet, Kuhn stressed the importance of local control over library policies, keeping the decisions concerning Internet policies as close as possible to the citizens who fund and use our libraries. He eloquently outlined a democracy's need for public libraries, the importance of local control, citizens' preference for more, rather than less, information, and those individuals' rights to decide what information they want for themselves or for their own children. The General Assembly eventually did provide funding for OPLIN without requiring filters in public libraries, a victory for our citizens' First Amendment rights.

The Future of Ohio's Libraries
Steve Wood

IN 1982, RACHEL NELSON, THEN DIRECTOR of the Cleveland Heights-University Heights Public Library, wrote an article entitled "The Medium-Sized Public Library in 2002." This article was so remarkably on target that it gives one hope as we look to the future of Ohio's libraries over the next twenty years. Perhaps it *is* possible to extrapolate a logical future from what we see around us today.

One sentence from Nelson's article truly resonates and, in considering our libraries today, may be the most important idea from that earlier article: "The ability to produce hard-copy information found online will be a welcome service." In thinking about 2023, our future twenty years hence, this sentence may remain one of several driving factors of what has yet to come.

Funding

While this chapter deals with the future of Ohio's libraries, "as Ohio goes, so goes the nation." The changes we see affecting us are the same as those affecting libraries all across the country. But today, what makes Ohio different from other states, as far as public libraries are concerned, is our willingness to provide funding on a statewide level. The Library and Local Government Support Fund (LLGSF) has, as its core, the desire to equalize funding throughout the state so that the quality of library service is less dependent on the size and relative wealth of the community. Ohio's funding for libraries is unique and ranks number one nationally. Circulation in our libraries reached 12.76 items per capita in 2000, while across the country the figure was only 6.44 items.

At the time of this writing, our economy, both nationally and in Ohio, is experiencing the worst downturn we have seen in a number of years. Not surprisingly, library funding in Ohio is suffering accordingly. With seventy-four percent of all public libraries in the state having the LLGSF as their sole source of revenue, downturns of this nature can be catastrophic—and while that will change in the short term, it has consequences over the long term.

An unpleasant possibility for future funding could easily be away from the LLGSF and toward much greater local support. The fact that this could easily eliminate the philosophy of equalization, so much a part of the LLGSF distribution formula, could carry little weight with the state legislature. And since many communities in Ohio are unable to generate support for local property tax levies, library service statewide is likely to deteriorate. A fact for the future is that less income for libraries could increase interest in consolidation of library systems. Can small public libraries afford not to join with other libraries in their area?

Buildings

The key to much of what we think about when we consider the future of libraries has to do with the library buildings themselves. What will they be like? Larger? Smaller? High tech? Low? It seems reasonable to assume that the newer buildings of today will still be around in twenty years or so, but we will be seeing new buildings built then that reflect an even further future.

Technology implies several trends that will directly affect libraries and library buildings in the future. First of all, electronic databases are available remotely. This trend will certainly continue. As long as there is a market for a particular database, you can be assured it will be available to purchase. Libraries are primary aggregators of electronic databases today, and, thanks to OPLIN, all libraries in the state have free access to a basic suite of services covering all topics and all ages. Many libraries also select additional databases deemed necessary to meet the needs of their specific communities—and pay for them themselves. This trend can only grow.

A word about online catalogs. It is truly disappointing that in the twenty-five to thrity years of significant automation, many libraries haven't grown beyond just replicating the old card catalogs we eliminated so handily. For those of us old enough to remember, the bibliographic records printed on the cards used in those catalogs, were constrained by man-made limitations such as two to five subject headings and formats relying on set rules. While automation completely eliminates those constraints, today's online catalog had grown only by adding keyword searching by author, title and subject (still only two to five) and the occasional analyzing of contents. What this implies is that the online catalog remains a librarian's tool generally inexplicable to the people we serve. I believe this will change (thankfully) and we will see a movement toward library catalogs looking, and acting, much more like Google and Amazon.com. When this happens, our collections become immediately more accessible to our customers.

A second trend, twenty-four-hour-a-day, seven-day-a-week, online reference service, is having an important impact on the way libraries function. For example, by mid-2003, KnowItNow, created by the Cleveland Public Library for the CLEVNET consortium, is gaining acceptance within the service areas of the thirty-one member libraries in northeast Ohio. Indeed, libraries in other parts of the state, including Worthington, Dayton, and Greene County, among others, have joined with CLEVNET and are providing 24/7 online reference service to their customers as well. A statewide 24/7 service can't be far away.

A third trend is that public libraries today are often the only source for their communities' access to personal computers and/or fast Internet connections. While PCs seem (today) slow in coming to rural and urban areas, this is not the case with suburban communities where home PC use is growing rapidly. For the future, it is not impossible to imagine that PCs, connected to high speed, broadband Internet (or whatever takes its place) will become as ubiquitous as the telephone. If future PC accessibility replicates what we currently see with telephones, what role, if any, will libraries play in Internet connectivity?

A fourth technology trend that will affect libraries relates to electronic publishing. The method of reading—paper or electronic—may not be as important as the method of publishing. Today, books in a paper format are published in limited quantities because of the expense of maintaining warehouses of inventory. This means that a book must be purchased quickly or it will go out of print. Should a person become interested in a specific title long after publishing, they must hope that their library had the foresight and money to purchase it, and that it hasn't been subsequently damaged, withdrawn, or stolen. How much more efficient (read cost-effective) to print a copy of a book *when it is actually wanted.*

Electronic publishing is operational today. We see an example of it every time someone prints out a full-text magazine article. There are a growing number of electronic journals available, usually for a fee, over the Internet. Today, these journals are esoteric and/or very expensive, but this is where magazine and newspaper publishing is going for all but the most popular, general interest titles—and maybe those as well.

Books, on the other hand, are more complex than magazines. Most book publishers are slow to move beyond the philosophical issues of electronic publishing, much less the technical. Insuring that publishers make a profit, including one-time and residual payments to authors, is just as complex as how to print out an entire book quickly and efficiently and at a cost that is not prohibitive. Stephen King's *Riding the Bullet* may be forgettable as literature, but it *will* be remembered as the first book to be published only in electronic format. The idea of a high-speed printer available in the library (bookstores too) that prints a complete book while the requestor waits is not beyond the realm of possibility. Experiments with this kind of technology are taking place today. But if we can print it out in the library for a customer, why can't we deliver it directly to their home or office?

Electronic distribution of books to home PCs, laptops, hand-held devices and personal data assistants (PDAs) is growing and the electronic publishing industry for books is growing accordingly. Is reading a book on an LCD screen catching on? And has the "right" reading device yet to be created? Is that the trend for the future or will we see growth of print on demand? Or both?

What we see as the future for books is little different for audio and video media. Since they are also available on the Internet today, it is reasonable to assume that all the copyright problems of today will be resolved and they will be available for downloading far into the future. Of even greater interest, perhaps, is how do we determine what materials and formats will be available through libraries? Until the middle of the twentieth century, it was a rare library that circulated more than books, magazines, and newspapers. But in 1948 the Cleveland Public Library established the first educational film circuit, setting the stage for libraries being about more than just books. After that we saw phonograph records, 8MM movies, videocassettes, art prints, realia, and even toys become staples in libraries. Today we have DVDs replacing videotapes, exactly as CDs replaced phonograph records. Certainly other changes in format may be based more on the Internet and its ability to provide information directly.

So what do these trends really mean for libraries? If remotely accessed electronic databases, fewer PCs, 24/7 online reference service and electronic publishing on demand truly catch on, will we operate in the future as we do today? Will we need buildings to house our staff, our reference areas, our collections, our PCs, or can we be much, much smaller than we are today? Will people have a reason to visit libraries in this future dominated by technology and whatever the Internet morphs into? My suspicion is *yes*, because there is another trend growing in libraries that demands increased space rather than decreased.

Public libraries have always developed programming, especially for children, and have perceived themselves as "community centers" for their service area and beyond. The extent of this perception is rapidly growing. The Internet and television tend to isolate people and many see libraries bringing people together in defense of, or in rebellion to, this isolation. Libraries are looking for ways to economically expand the programming they offer to all ages in their communities and this will certainly grow. It fits nicely with the philosophy expressed in Ohio's statewide public relations campaign from a number of years ago, LIBRARIES: LEARNING FOR LIFE. Nothing says it better.

Staffing

In the aggregate, these trends seem to imply that although library buildings may remain the same size, perhaps grow because of the community center/programming focus, libraries will likely expand. At the same time, the need for library space for what we currently consider as "traditional" services (information and educational/recreational reading/listening/viewing materials) is likely to decrease. If this occurs, what does this mean for library staffing?

For the past several years, we have heard that the number of professional librarians (holding an MLS) is decreasing and soon there will not be enough to go around. But if both information *and* library materials can be provided electronically to the customer at home or office, and there is little need for them to make a visit to the library building for these services, what will keep us from greater and greater consolidation of library systems as a way of becoming much more cost effective? And if that occurs, will we need staff at the educational levels currently predicted? If what predominately happens at a library building is programming, won't we need increasing numbers of paraprofessionals rather than increasing numbers of professionals? To staff centralized online information centers, a case could be made for a much more specialized, more technical, degree than our current one-year master's level degree in library and information science. At the same time, won't we want to insure that the programming we create reaches the largest possible audiences? Outreach to nursing homes, senior housing, and remote parts of cities and counties will continue to take place, in addition to what occurs in library buildings.

If you are a traditionalist, some of the concepts in these pages may strike you as grim, but that is really not the case. Libraries always reinvent themselves, keeping pace with the times and with what their constituency desire from them. That will not change.

What I envision for our future is the public library serving two primary functions. It will be the distribution point for both information resources and whatever constitutes "free" availability of reading/viewing/listening materials. How a "local" library is constituted remains to be seen but it seems logical that consolidation, major or minor, will certainly take place.

And second, library buildings, many existing today and more that will be built, will serve as a local community's hub, the central source for quality programming. Increasingly, people will want opportunities to come together with their friends and neighbors for the life-long education and entertainment, for the music and literary discussions, and for the free exchange of ideas that will take place within our walls.

In truth, isn't that what libraries have always been about?

Cornerstones and Landmarks in Ohio Library History*

Jay Ladd

TWO HUNDRED DATES WHICH ARE CORNERSTONES and landmarks in Ohio library history is our bicentennial tribute to the dedicated people who helped build and sustain our Ohio libraries. We can trace our first Ohio library back to 1796. From this early date to the present the interest in the development and activities of Ohio libraries has been significant.

Prior to 1817, when Ohio's first general library legislation was passed, some twenty libraries were incorporated by special laws.(1) By 1850 the state had incorporated 192 library societies, 64 lyceums, institutes, athenaeums, and literary societies, 23 college literary societies, and 12 miscellaneous educational agencies.(2) The seventh U.S. Census, 1850, counted 65 public libraries, 13 school libraries, 248 Sunday school libraries, 22 college libraries, and 4 church libraries in existence. In *Sketches of Ohio Libraries*, published in 1902, over 400 libraries are listed to be in existence by 1900. By 1975 the Ohio Directory of Libraries lists 250 public tax supported libraries, 1,828 public school library/media centers, 115 libraries in post secondary educational institutions, 44 institution libraries, 123 special libraries, and The State Library for a total of 2,361 libraries. To list a date or more for each of the libraries would result in a volume or two. While the author has collected more than 500 "important" dates, it may seem

---

*Reprinted from the Ohio Library Association BULLITEN, *Building on Our Heritage*, October 1976

arbitrary to select only 200 dates for this article. However, in order to have a diversity of coverage the following guidelines were used:
1. Listing of all the libraries established between 1796 and 1808.
2. Listing of at least today's twelve largest public libraries.
3. Listing of at least today's twelve largest academic libraries.
4. Listing of *first* specialized libraries.
5. Listing of *firsts* in special services provided by libraries.
6. Listing of important legislation.
7. Listing of library organizations.
8. Listing of significant publications.
9. Listing of *firsts* in related professional fields.
10. Listing of *first* libraries in the largest cities.
Hopefully these dates and the list of references will encourage others to do further, needed research in Ohio library history.

Significant Dates in Ohio Library History

1793 • The first press in Ohio was established at Cincinnati by William Maxwell. On November 9 he issued the first number of "The Centinel of the North-Western Territory." The first book printed in Ohio was the *Laws of the Territory of the United States North-West of the Ohio*, known as "Maxwell's Code," which also came from his press, in 1796. (53,107)

1796 • Putnam Family Library, first circulating collection of books in Ohio, was established by an Association formed by Colonel Israel Putnam at Belpre, near Marietta. Afterwards known as Belpre Farmer's Library and still later as the Belpre Library. Existed until 1815. (51,71,107)

1802 • Circulating library was projected and organized in Cincinnati on March 6 and existed for a very short time. L. Kerr was the librarian. (33,51)

1802 • David Hudson and George Kilbourne formed a subscription library in Hudson which developed into the Hudson Library and Historical Society. (27)

1803 • Erie Literary Society, Burton, in the Western Reserve was the first academy to be incorporated. (2)

1803 • Worthington Public Library traces its origins to the organization and founding of the Stanbery Library in Worthington . (24,110)

1804 • The Coonskin Library, best known early Ohio Library, was founded by the Western Library Association at Ames. Incorporated on February 19, 1810, as the Western Library Association. (31,51, 107)

1805 • The Social Library Society of Dayton was incorporated by a legislative act, the first recognition of libraries in the laws of the state. (56,107)

1807 • Granville Alexandrian Society Library became the second library to be incorporated in the state. (9)

1807 • *Halcyon Itinerary and True Millenium Messenger*, first magazine published in Ohio at Marietta. (21)

1807 • Poland Library Society formed. Incorporated by the state in 1810. First documented library in the Western Reserve territory. (42,56)

1811 • Cleveland's first Library Association formed with Dr. David Long, Cleveland's first physician and surgeon as its first librarian. (12)

1812 • The first bookseller in Cincinnati to stake his success on the sales of books and stationery alone was John Corson. In August 1813 he opened a circulating library in his store. (97)

1815 • Cincinnati Lancaster Seminary incorporated by the state on February 4 and opened on April 17, 1815. In 1819 incorporated as Cincinnati College. (87,97)

1816 • Columbus Literary Society, the earliest Columbus library company held its first meeting on April 8, 1816. (24)

1816 • *Systematic Catalogue of Books Belonging to the Circulation Library Society of Cincinnati* published. Probably the earliest printed library catalogue in Ohio. (98)

1817 • General law was passed providing for the incorporation of library companies and schools. (9)

1817 • Ohio State Library founded. First library in Ohio supported by public funds. First librarian was John L. Harper. (9)

1818 • Society of Natural History Library, Cincinnati traces its development to the founding of the Cincinnati Museum. (115)

1819 • Medical College of Ohio, the oldest medical school west of the Alleghenies, was incorporated by an act of the legislature and organized a year later. Opened its doors in 1821 and the library was founded in 1826. In 1896 it joined with the University of Cincinnati. (78,87,97)

1819 • Ohio University Library founded. However, Ohio University was incorporated in 1802 under the name of the American Western University. In 1804, a second act of incorporation changed its name to Ohio University. It was the first institution of higher learning in the Northwest Territory. (41,56)

1820 • First real bookstore, Cleveland Book Store, opened in June by Herschel Foote. (58)

1820 • Horace J. Hulbert opened the first bindery in Cleveland. (58)

1822 • Historical Society of Ohio was incorporated on February 1 by the state. (49)

1823 • First catalogue of the State Library of Ohio published. In 1826 the second catalogue of books was printed. (105)

1824 • Miami University Library, Oxford founded. The first appropriation for books was made in 1825. In 1803 an act to provide for the locating of a college township was passed and in 1809 the act to establish the university was passed. (54,56)

1824 • Ohio General Assembly passed the first library law which provided for the appointment of a librarian for the State Library by the legislature. The appointment was for a three year term at an annual salary of $200. (9)

1824 • Theological Seminary of the Protestant Episcopal Church in the Diocese of Ohio incorporated by the state. The original act was supplemented in 1826 which established the name Kenyon College. The seminary has a library collection which is known today as the Colburn Library. Kenyon College Library founded in 1865. (91)

1826 • Western Reserve College Library, Hudson, founded. Moved to Cleveland in 1882 and the name changed to Adelbert College. In 1884 incorporated as Western Reserve University. (14)

1826 • Cincinnati Academy of Fine Arts founded and incorporated by the state in 1828. (56,87)

1829 • Ohio Mechanics' Institute Library, Cincinnati established. The collection, years later, became part of the public library. (111)

1831 • Denison University Library founded. The first item on the accession list was dated October 28, 1831. (59)

1831 • Erodelphian Society of Miami University incorporated. It was the first college literary society to be so incorporated by the state. (56)

1831 • Historical and Philosophical Society of Ohio was incorporated. The society was formally organized in Columbus. In 1849 this society, with its library was moved from Columbus to Cincinnati in order to form a union with the Historical Society of Cincinnati. (49)

1833 • *Catalogue of the Books Contained in the Library of Miami University: Arranged According to Subject*, published by W.W. Bishop. Probably the first printed catalogue of books of an Ohio college library. (20)

1833 • Cleveland Library Company secured a state charter of incorporation. Was Cleveland's first subscription library. (56)

1834 • Akron Lyceum and Library Association granted charter by the state. Earliest library on record in the village of Akron. (116)

1834 • Oberlin College Library founded. The college was established in 1833. (103)

1834 • Winthrop B. Smith founded the firm of Truman and Smith in Cincinnati which soon became one of the largest textbook houses in the world. They published the seven volumes of *McGuffey Eclectic Reader*. First volume published in 1836 and as of 1976, 270,000,000 copies have been sold. (93,102)

1835 • Young Men's Mercantile Library Association of Cincinnati incorporated. Still in existence today. (56)

1835 • Marietta College Library was founded when the present college charter was obtained. (78)

1837 • Lane Theological Seminary Library founded. Lane Seminary was established in 1829 and opened in 1832. (39)

1837 • Muskingum College chartered with facilities for a library. (2)

1838 • Toledo's first library was organized by the Toledo Young Men's Association under a charter from the state. Had original membership of 66. In 1864 reorganized and became the Toledo Library Association. This subscription library was the beginning of the Toledo Public Library which was established by the 1873 Library Law. Library Association transferred all its property. (99)

1842 • Ohio Wesleyan University Library started. College was granted charter by the state on March 7. A preparatory school was going in 1842 with a college faculty. Classes organized by 1844 with a fairly well stocked bookcase as the students' library. (113)

1844 • Cincinnati Historical Society organized. In 1849 the society was united with the State Historical Society. (107)

184 • Ohio State Library opened to the public for the first time. (24)

1845 • Wittenberg University Library founded when the university was incorporated. (31)

1846 • First Ohio Public School Library Law passed which enacted permissive legislation whereby each school district of the state was authorized to raise money for the purpose of establishing and maintaining a common school library. (2)

1846 • Ohio Penitentiary Library came into recognition. In 1854 library received first state aid from legislature. (77)

1847 • Cincinnati Law Library Association Library founded. The first law library founded west of the Allegheny Mountains. (115)

1847 • Otterbein College founded. College had no library until 1857 (10,78)

1848 • Cleveland Library Association incorporated. This was formed by the "second" Young Men's Literary Association which was established in 1846. In 1880 name changed to the Case Library and in 1924 the library affiliated with Western Reserve University. (27,42)

1850 • Western Reserve Eclectic Institute secured a special charter from the General Assembly. The College had a nucleus of the library in existence by 1854. In 1867 Board of Trustees changed the name to Hiram College. (72,81)

1851 • *Ohio Farmer* founded at Cleveland by Thomas Brown. This journal is still being published today. (60)

1853 • Antioch College incorporated and opened on October 6. In 1852 there was an appeal for books and funds for the library. (55)

1853 • Cincinnati Public Library incorporated. Collection began as result of the Ohio School Library Law. Opened to the public in July 1856. (9)

1853 • Cleveland Public Library traces its start to the Ohio School Library Law of 1853 when Central High School received a collection of 2,200 books. This collection became the nucleus for the Public School Library which opened to the public in 1869. In 1883 the name was changed to Cleveland Public Library. The library opened with approximately 5,800 books. (27)

1853 • Ohio School Library Act passed which marks the beginning of the free public library movement in Ohio. The law provided for an annual levy of one-tenth mill on all the taxable property of the state. Abolished in 1860. (9)

1856 • Cincinnati Public Library Art Department began. In 1872 opened a special room, called the Art Room. (9)

1860 • Dayton Public Library formed as a combination of Dayton Library Association and Dayton Public School Library. The Dayton Public School Library was established under the Ohio School Library Law of 1853 and opened in 1855. (9,19)

1860 • The Law Library which had until this time been a part of the State Library was removed to separate quarters in the State House and was called The Supreme Court of Ohio Law Library. (9)

1864 • Lloyd Library and Museum, Cincinnati was founded by John Uri Lloyd. This library is one of the ten leading assemblages of plant science literature in the United States. (115)

1864 • Toledo Library Association founded. This subscription library was the beginning of the Toledo Public Library which was established by the 1873 Library Law. (9)

1866 • Akron Library Association incorporated. This library developed into the Akron Public Library by 1874. (106)

1866 • Lane Public Library, Hamilton opened. In 1868 Clark Lane executed a deed of conveyance of all library property of the Lane Free Library to the Hamilton City Council for the use of the public. (16)

1867 • Ohio College Association founded. Later included a Librarians Section which reorganized into the Academic Library Association of Ohio—ALAO in 1973. (101)

1867 • The Western Reserve and Northern Ohio Historical Society founded. The library was equipped and opened to the public in 1871. (109)

1869 • William Frederick Poole appointed librarian, Cincinnati Public Library at a salary of $2,500. Was at Cincinnati until 1874. (114)

1870 • Cincinnati General Hospital Library established. Largest and oldest medical library in the city. (115)

1870 • Ohio State University was incorporated as the Ohio Agricultural and Mechanical College. When it opened in 1873 it had a separate library. In 1878 changed its name. (89)

1870 • University of Cincinnati established by law on April 16 and opened for classes in 1873. Prior the institution was known as McMicken University which was founded in 1859. (87)

1871 • Cincinnati Public Library opened on Sundays starting on March 12. First large municipal library to make its facilities available on the Sabbath. (114)

1872 • Buchtel College with the Bierce Library opened. The college became the University of Akron in 1913. (25)

1872 • Youngstown Public Library began as a combination of a school and a subscription library. (100)

1873 • Booksellers Protective Union was founded in Cincinnati. Soon developed into the American Book Trade Union and then into the American Book Trade Association. (46)

1873 • Public Library and Reading Room of Columbus opened. This library developed into the present Columbus Public Library. (2,71)

1878 • The combined collection of Bishops Payne and Arnett formed the nucleus of the first black library collection in Ohio at Wilberforce University. (29)

1879 • Cincinnati Public Library established its first branch library at Cumminsville. The first city in Ohio to do so. (9,111)

1880 • Dayton Public Library introduced dictionary card cataloging, the fourth of its kind in the country. Constructed by Electra C. Doren, Assistant Librarian; published in 1884. (19)

1882 • American Library Association held its first meeting in Ohio at Cincinnati, May 24–27 with 47 in attendance, Justin Winsor, presiding. ALA had a total of 454 members that year. It met for the second time in Cincinnati in 1940 with 3056 attending. In 1896 ALA met for the first time in Cleveland, September 1–8 with 363 attending and John Cotton Dana presiding. In 1950 and 1961 ALA also held its annual conferences in Cleveland. (4)

1884 • Canton Public Library Association incorporated. Is now Stark County District Library. (112)

1884 • Cleveland Public Library began the issuing of teachers' cards entitling the holder to draw five books at one time. First library in Ohio and second in the country to do so. In 1887 the library sent the first collection of books to a school and termed them a classroom library. (23,27)

1885 • Ohio Archeological and Historical Society organized. (49)

1887 • Mansfield Public Library was incorporated as the Memorial Library Association of Mansfield. (71)

1888 • Youngstown University Library traces its beginning to the Youngstown Association School founding. In 1908 School of Law organized which was the beginning of college level instruction. (82)

1890 • Warder Public Library, Springfield opened. This library was the outgrowth of the Springfield Library Association. Library was incorporated in 1872. (6,71)

1890 • William Howard Brett inaugurated open shelf system in the Cleveland Public Library which was the first large public library to adopt and successfully maintain it. (9,27)

1892 • Cleveland Public Library opened its first branch of the system, West Side Branch. (27)

1892 • Rowfant Club, Cleveland founded. First club in Ohio devoted exclusively to the arts of the book. (46)

1892 • United States Circuit Court of Appeals library founded by William Howard Taft. (92)

1895 • Ohio Library Association organized. The association was the idea of W.H. Brett, Electra C. Doren and Linda Eastman. Brett was the first president and first meeting was held in Cleveland. (68)

1896 • Cleveland Public Library opened the first high school library branch in the Central High School—one of the first in the country. (47)

1896 • *Cumulative Index to Periodicals* founded by W.H. Brett and edited by the Cleveland Public Library and published by the Helman-Taylor Company, Cleveland. (58)

1896 • Dayton Public Library opened one of the earliest and successful in-service training programs for librarians, under Electra C. Doren. The first to be established in any Ohio Library and one of the first in the United States. (9)

1896 • An Ohio law was passed which changed entirely the administration of the Ohio State Library and placed it under the control of a new Board of Commissioners. At the Board's first meeting they elected Charles B. Galbreath, State Librarian. At subsequent meetings during the year rules and regulations were adopted that opened the State Library, on equal terms, to all citizens of the state. (71)

1896 • Traveling Library Department of the State Library was established. The first traveling library was sent to a women's club in Mt. Vernon. Charles Galbreath was the father of the traveling library system in Ohio. (33)

1896 • William Howard Brett elected president of The American Library Association. First librarian from Ohio to hold the office. (4)

1897 • Cleveland Public Library organized the Children's Library League, the first of many such organizations in the nation. (27)

1897 • First list of Ohio State publications was published with Rutherford B. Hayes, editor. In 1964 the first published union list of Ohio documents was issued. (105)

1898 • Cleveland Public Library opened its first separate children's room at the main library. Effie Power was its first librarian. (27)

1898 • County library legislation was first passed in the state when county libraries were created in Hamilton and Van Wert Counties. The Brumback Library was the first county library in the world. The gift of a library building required new legislation to be enacted. The library was functioning by 1901. (32,33)

1899 • Cincinnati Public Library extended its services to all residents of Hamilton County when it established its first stations in June. (32)

1899 • East Liverpool Public Library and the Steubenville Public Library were the first libraries in Ohio to receive Carnegie grants of $50,000 and $62,000 respectively. (15)

1900 • Cincinnati Library Society for the Blind was organized with the librarian as president. (9)

1900 • Dayton Public Library began weekly announcements of new books and articles about the library in the city newspapers. (9)

1900 • First professionally trained black librarian in Ohio, Edward Christopher Williams, received his library degree from New York State Library School. He was also the librarian of the Hatch Library, Western Reserve and helped found the Ohio Library Association and establish the Western Reserve Library School. (43)

1901 • Cincinnati Public Library began a Story Hour Program on Saturday mornings. (111)

1901 • Toledo Public Library started a small rental collection of current fiction. First free public library in Ohio to adopt the plan of renting books. (9)

1902 • Cincinnati Public Library received a gift of $180,000 from Carnegie for the building of six branches. (9)

1902 • Harrison Act was passed which was the most liberal in its general application and tax rate of any law up to this time. It authorized school boards to establish and maintain public libraries in cities, villages or special school districts. This law was the fourth general school district law. 1853 first; 1867 second; 1898 third. (9)

1902 • *Sketches of Ohio Libraries* published by Ohio Board of Library Commissioners and compiled by C.B. Galbreath, State Librarian. (71)

1903 • Cleveland Public Library, Library for the Blind established with a small collection of books. The work with the blind was formally organized as the Department for the Blind in 1906. (9)

1903 • Western Reserve University Library School founded. Received a grant of $100,000 from Andrew Carnegie. School opened in October 1904 and the first class of 12 graduated in June 1905. In 1923 the school received an additional $25,000 from Carnegie Corporation in recognition of the school's success. In 1949 the first M.S. degree in Library Science was awarded. (30)

1904 • First *Library Laws of Ohio* in Force, was published. (105)

1906 • Establishment of a law which created within the State Library the Office of Library Organizer. This position was designed to provide professional viewpoint to those communities desiring to establish a library or improve their library service to the community. First annual report made in 1909, by Mary E. Downey. (13)

1907 • Chemical Abstracts Service founded. Moved to the Ohio State University campus in 1909. World's largest secondary information service in chemistry and chemical engineering. (8)

1908 •Cleveland Public Library opened Perkins House, the first branch in the United States devoted to children only. (27)

1910 • Legislative Reference Department of the Ohio State Library was established by an act of the Ohio legislature. (9)

1910 • Ohio Library Association district meetings were instituted by Mary E. Downey. (84)

1912 • Cleveland Public Library developed an extensive hospital library service with the opening of a deposit and delivery station in a room of the Cleveland State Hospital for the Insane. (9)

1913 • Cleveland Public Library organized its main collection on a subject division basis with a subject specialist in charge of each. (108)

1913 • Kent State Normal began with a room for the library. In 1929 the David Ladd Rockwell Library was inaugurated, the same week Kent State College came into being. (1)

1914 • Bowling Green State University Library founded. (5)

1916 • Rutherford B. Hayes Library dedicated. (92)

1917 • University of Toledo Library was organized as a department of the university. (37)

1919 • Cleveland plant of E.I. du Pont de Nemours and Co. Library established. One of the oldest technical libraries in a private firm. (108)

1921 • The first professional librarian, Herbert S. Hirshberg, appointed to the position of librarian of the Ohio State Library. (26)

1921 • County Library District Law passed which provided for the establishment of county libraries upon petition and a favorable vote. Cuyahoga County Library was first established under this law. (9,28)

1923 • Dayton Public Library began a book wagon service for distributing books to school branches and to stations in Dayton. The first city in Ohio to utilize such a service. First book wagon carried 600 volumes and cost $623.04. (9)

1923 • First *Directory of Ohio Libraries* published by the Ohio State Library. (105)

1925 • Cincinnati Public Library began a weekly radio book talk program from station WKRC. (9)

1927 • Cleveland Chapter of Special Libraries Association was officially welcomed into the association. In 1930 the Special Libraries Association of Cincinnati became a chapter of SLA. (22,40)

1927 • Western Reserve University Library School awarded its first bachelor of library science degree. (86)

1928 • University of Dayton Library founded. (5)

1929 • Business Information Bureau, Cleveland Public Library began its regular service with Rose Vormelker as its head. In January 1930 the first issue of Business Information Sources was published. (27)

1929 • Martha Kinney Cooper Ohioana Library founded by Mrs. Myers Y. Cooper and named after its founder. It is a private research and reference library open to the public. (36)

1930 • *Library Service for Children* by Effie Louise Power was published by the American Library Association. It was the first authoritative work on the subject. Miss Power was the first children's librarian at the Cleveland Public Library. (27)

1930 • Ohio Library Trustees Association organized in Dayton with Mr. Charles R. Wilson of Stow as its first president. (68)

1931 • Ohio County Intangible Tax Law passed. Fathered by Robert A. Taft, then a State Senator. (61)

1931 • *The Ohio Library Association BULLETIN*, first issue, April 1931. (67)

1931 Cincinnati Public Library and the Cleveland Public were selected to act as regional distributing center for supplying free books for the blind. (93)

1933 • First separate book trailer began in Clark County, Ohio. It was a cooperative venture by the District YWCA, Springfield and Ohio State Library and Warder Public Library who provided the books. (18)

1935 • Euclid Public Library established. (45)

1935 • $100,000 was approved by the Ohio legislature for state aid to libraries. This was accomplished through the efforts of the state librarian Paul A.T. Noon and his enthusiastic co-workers, plus friends of the state aid program. Program administered by State Library. (61)

1936 • Cleveland Regional Union Catalog was established as a WPA project. (68)

1936 • *Regional List of Serials in the College and University Libraries in Ohio* published. List also contains Code of Practice for Interlibrary Loans Between College and University Libraries in Ohio and Union Subject List of Special Libraries in Ohio College, University and Seminary Libraries, 1935, compiled by Gertrude Wulfe-koetter. This list is one of the earliest attempts of cooperation between college and university libraries in Ohio. Twenty-six libraries participated. (66)

1937 • Work began on the Union Catalog at the Ohio State Library. The first state in the nation to have a centralized union catalog of the holdings of the largest public libraries in its state. Catalog housed at the State Library, Columbus. (57)

1941 • Cleveland Public Library began the first reported library service to shut-ins. The library received an endowment of $450,000 from the Judd estate. The income was to be used for the service. (27)

1942 • *County Library Primer* by Mildred Sandoe was published. Sandoe was appointed in 1935 to the position of state library organizer and during 1935–36 she made extensive surveys of Ohio libraries. (62,80)

1942 • Ohio Library Association's program of awards and honors began with the establishment of the Trustee Award. Mrs. Elsie Bennett Wilson won this first award. In 1960 the James O. Amos Family won the first Citizens Award. In 1963 Helen Sunnafrank won the first Librarian of the Year Award. In 1970 Carl Vitz, Cincinnati was the first librarian named to the OLA Hall of Fame. Mrs. Elsie Bennett Wilson was the first trustee to be so honored. In 1970 Judith Mowery won the first OLA Bulletin Best Article of the Year Award and in 1972 Jacqueline Johns won the first Diana Vescelius Award. (7)

1946 • Live Long and Like It Library Club, Cleveland Public Library organized by Dr. Fern Long. The first in the nation with a program for senior citizens primarily interested in an educational experience rather than programs of pure recreation. (27)

1947 • County District Library Law passed. Permitted any county resident to use any public library in the county. (61)

1947 • Ohio Association of School Librarians was organized by more than 100 school librarians meeting in Toledo. (68)

1948 • Cleveland Public Library began the first educational film circuit in Ohio. They distributed 16mm to 10 Ohio libraries in a regional area surrounding the City. (11)

1949 • Kent State University School of Library Science began offering graduate courses. Was accredited in 1963 and achieved school status in 1966. (52)

1950 • First Ohio Library Association scholarship granted. (79)

1953 • Inter-University Library Council formed with its members, the librarians of the state supported universities of Ohio. (68)

1953 • Lorain County Librarians' Association was formed. This was a beginning of recent cooperative activities in the area which developed into INFO, a library consortia for Lorain and Medina counties. (38)

1953 • Supreme Court of Ohio decided that a 1951 amendment to the law meant that the county budget commission must decide on the basis of "the needs of libraries" and not the needs of libraries in relation to other units. This decision established the priority of public libraries in claiming revenue from the intangibles tax. (79)

1954 • Ohio Library Association brief was influential in the Ohio Supreme Court's decision to uphold public libraries' "prior claim" to intangibles taxes over those of other bodies. (68)

1954 • Program of Doctor of Philosophy in Librarianship initiated at Western Reserve University School of Library Science. In 1959 Miss Jean E. Lowrie received the first Ph.D. (86)

1955 • Center for Documentation and Communication Research, School of Library Science, Western Reserve University began a five year study. This was a pioneering venture that resulted in the development of basic principles for the analysis of information for computer retrieval. (86)

1955 • Cincinnati and Hamilton County Public Library inaugurated a drive-in service. (3)

1956 • Ohio State Library established rural library service centers and bookmobile programs from funds made available from the Library Services Act of 1956. (68)

1958 • First issue of *News From the State Library of Ohio* issued in February. (105)

1962 • *Ohio Authors and Their Books; Biographical Data and Selective Biographies for Ohio Authors, Natives and Residents, 1796–1950*; edited by William Coyle and published by World Publishing Co. (105)

1962 • Southwestern Ohio Rural Libraries Council founded (SWORL). In 1968 received LSA Title I funds. (38,50)

1963 • Ohio Library Foundation was founded in January "to aid any college, public, school or special library." (65)

1963 • Wyman W. Parker's *Possibility of Extensive Academic Library Cooperation in Ohio; A Survey* was published by the Ohio College Association. (75)

1964 • Ohio Library Association and Ohio Library Trustee Association joint Executive Office established with A. Chapman Parsons as its first executive director. (76)

1965 • Ohio State Library began taking new steps towards sound library development from funds made available from the Library Services and Construction Act of 1965. (68)

1966 • Trotwood Branch of the Dayton and Montgomery County Public Library dedicated. First library building in Ohio to be completed with assistance from the Library Services and Construction Act. (64)

1967 • The libraries in the Ohio Valley area began as a viable unit. In 1969 the Ohio Valley Area Libraries (OVAL) was formed and in 1973 was established as Ohio's first ALSO. (38)

1967 • The Ohio Books/Jobs program operated by the Ohio State Library began. (73)

1967 • Ohio College Library Center was incorporated on July 6. First annual meeting was held at Denison University on 25 October. Frederick G. Kilgour appointed as executive director. Center opened its membership to non-academic libraries in 1973. (74,101)

1968 • Art Research Libraries of Ohio (ARLO) formed when funds were approved from Title III. (88)

1968 • First O.S.U. Library Standards and Planning Workshop held. (74)

1968 • Ohio Library Development Program approved by Ohio Library Association and the Ohio Trustees Association on October 19. Revised with minor nonsubstantive changes by the OLA Library Development Committee, February 1974. (69)

1968 • First Library Executive Development Program for head librarians, held at Miami University, Oxford. (48)

1968 • *Survey of Ohio Libraries and State Library Services* by Ralph Blasingame published. (13)

1969 • Inter-University Library Council Reference and Interlibrary Loan Service (IULC-RAILS) begun. (85)

1969 • Ohio General Assembly enacted the enabling legislation for the Ohio Library Development Plan. Governor Rhodes signed S.B. 262, August 26. (83)

1970 • First *Ohio Libraries*, newsletter of the OLA was issued. (79)

1970 • LSCA money used to assist multi-county library cooperatives. This led to the development of:
Central Ohio Interlibrary Network (COIN)—1971
Miami Valley Library Organization (MILO)—1970
Mideastern Ohio Library Organization (MOLO)—1971
Northwestern Library District (NORWELD)—1973
Northeastern Ohio Library Association (NOLA)—1972
Southeastern Ohio Library Organization (SOLO)—1970

1970 • Ohio Library Association Board of Directors adopted an "Intellectual Freedom Policy Statement," published in the *Ohio Library Association Bulletin* in January 1971. (79)

1970 • Ohio Library Association Hall of Fame for Librarians and Trustees was inaugurated. (79)

1970 • The Ohio State University Libraries' online automated circulation system became operational. The implementation marked the culmination of about three years of planning, design, and programming. (17)

1971 • Black Studies Library, Ohio State University established; the largest separate library of its kind in Ohio. (29)

1971 • *Financing Public Libraries in Ohio* by Frederick D. Stocker published by Ohio Library Foundation. (96)

1971 • First Ohio Archives Library Institute held at the new Ohio Historical Center in Columbus. (34)

1972 • Ohio Library Association's Standards for the Public Libraries of Ohio was approved by the Board of Directors. (79)

1972 • TWX Interlibrary Loan Network (TWXIL) began operation. (104)

1973 • New Health Sciences Library, Ohio State University opened with the world's largest Randtriever. (44)

1973 • State Library of Ohio Microfilm Automated Catalog (SLOMAC) began operations. (95)

1974 • First Ohio Governor's Conference on Library and Information Services held in Columbus on April 2. (90)

1974 • *Recommended Job Classifications and Salary Goals for Ohio Academic, Public, School Libraries* was published by the Ohio Library Association. This was an update of previous studies, 1967–1971 and the first time academic and school libraries were included. (70)

1975 • A.J. Goldwyn's *Toward Tomorrow's Area Library Service* study published. (38)

1975 • First grant of money was given to initiate Ohio's METRO development plan (Metropolitan library system). Cuyahoga County Public Library received $4,000 for a grant from federal Library Services and Construction Act funds. On November 28, Ohio General Assembly passed Senate Bill 257 which authorizes metropolitan library systems. (35)

1975 • Interlibrary Cooperation Planning Institute held at O.S.U.'s Center for Tomorrow, October 26–28. (74)

Sources

1) Charlcie Adams, "Kent State University Library," M.A. Thesis, Kent State University, 1950.

2) Frederic D. Aldrich, *The School Library in Ohio with Special Emphasis on its Legislative History*, New York, Scarecrow Press, 1959.

3) Emily Lou Alford, "Drive-in Service for Libraries," in *Encyclopedia of Library and Information Science*, New York, Marcel Dekker, 1972.

4) American Library Association, *Membership Directory*, Chicago, 1974.

5) *American Library Directory*, 29th edition, New York, Bowker, 1974.

6) Adah W. Arthur, "A History of the Warder Public Library, Springfield, Ohio." M.A. Thesis, Kent State University, 1955.

7) "Awards and Honors Program," Columbus, Ohio Library Association, 1975.

8) Dale B. Baker, "Chemical Abstract Service," in *Encyclopedia of Library and Information Service*, New York, Marcel Dekker, 1970.

9) Frances M. Battles, "An Account of the Development of the Public Library Movement in Ohio, with Special References to Some Outstanding Libraries," M.A. Thesis, University of Illinois, 1928.

10) Nancy C. Baughman, "A History of the Otterbein College Library," M.S. Thesis, Western Reserve University, 1955.

11) Virginia M. Beard, "Cleveland Heads 1st Film Circuit," *Library Journal*, 74 (March 15, 1949).

12) Elbert J. Benton, *Cultural Story of an American City: Cleveland, vol. 1: During the Log Cabin Phases 1796–1825*, Cleveland, Western Reserve Historical Society, 1943.

13) Ralph W. Blasingame, *Survey of Ohio Libraries and State Library Service*, Columbus, State Library of Ohio, 1968.

14) George S. Bobinski, "A Brief History of the Libraries of Western Reserve University, 1826–1952," M.S. Thesis, Western Reserve University, 1952.

15) George S. Bobinski, *Carnegie Libraries: Their History and Impact on American Public Library Development*, Chicago, American Library Association, 1969.

16) Clyde N. Bowden, "The History of Lane Public Library, Hamilton, Ohio," M.S. Thesis, Western Reserve University, 1955.

17) Lewis C. Branscomb, *Report of the Director of Libraries for the Fiscal Year 1970–1971*, Columbus, Ohio State University, 1971.

18) Eleanor F. Brown, *Bookmobiles and Bookmobile Service*, Scarecrow Press, 1967.

19) Ruth A. Buzzard, "History of Bookmobile Service, Dayton Public Library, Dayton, Ohio," M.S. Thesis, Western Reserve University, 1953.

20) *Catalogue of the Books Contained in the Library of Miami University: Arranged According to Subject*, Oxford, W.W. Bishop, 1833.

21) Richard R. Centing, "Ohio Magazines," *Ohioana Quarterly*, 17 (Fall 1974).

22) "Cincinnati [Annual Report]" *Special Libraries*, 21 (May–June 1930).

23) Cleveland Public Library, *The Work of the Cleveland Public Library with the Children and the Means Used to Reach Them*, Cleveland, 1910.

24) Lucile Clifton, "Beginnings of Literary Culture in Columbus, Ohio, 1812–1840," Ph.D. Dissertation, Ohio State University, 1948.

25) Ruth W. Clinefeller, "A History of Bierce Library of the University of Akron," M.A. Thesis, Kent State University, 1956.

26) Sidney Cohen, "Biographical Data on the Librarians of the Ohio State Library, 1817–1960," M.A. Thesis, Kent State University, 1961.

27) Jack C. Cramer, "History and Development of Library Service in the Township of Hudson, Summit County, Ohio," M.A. Thesis, Kent State University, 1950.

28) "Cuyahoga County Library," *Ohio Libraries*, 1 (June 1924).

29) Eleanor Daniel, Head, Black Studies Library, Ohio State University to Jay Ladd, Columbus, June 30, 1976.

30) Frederick B. Davenport, "A History of the Western Reserve University School, 1904–1954," M.S. Thesis, Western Reserve University, 1956.

31) Luella S. Eutsler, Reference Department, Wittenberg University to Jay Ladd, January 5, 1972.

32) "Existing County Libraries," *Ohio Libraries*, 1 (February 1927).

33) Elizabeth Faries, "The History of Libraries in Ohio," *Ohio Library Association BULLETIN*, 31 (April 1961).

34) "First Ohio Archives-Library Institute," *News From the State Library of Ohio*, 114 (December 18, 1970).

35) Kevin C. Flaherty, "Metropolitan Library Systems," *News From the State Library of Ohio*, 172 (April 16, 1976).

36) Bernice W. Foley, "Ohioana Library—One of a Kind," *Ohio Library Association BULLETIN*, 44 (April 1974).

37) Mary M. Gillham, *The University of Toledo Library, Annual Report*, 1966–67, Toledo, University of Toledo, 1967.

38) A.J. Goldwyn, *Toward Tomorrow's Area Library Service: A Survey of Regional Library Cooperation in Ohio: 1974*, Columbus, State Library of Ohio, 1975.

39) M.E. Hagemann, Secretary-Treasurer to the Trustees of the Lane Seminary to Jay Ladd, Columbus, June 14, 1972.

40) "Highlights of the Conference," *Special Libraries*, 18 (July–August, 1927).

41) Thomas N. Hoover, *The History of Ohio University*, Athens, Ohio University Press, 1954.

42) George Jones, "Materials Relating to the Development of a History of Public Libraries in the Western Reserve," M.A. Thesis, Kent State University, 1957.

43) E.J. Josey, *The Black Librarian in America*, Metuchen, Scarecrow Press, 1970.

44) Jay Ladd, "Annual Report, Head, Department Libraries, 1972/73," Columbus, 1973 (Mimeographed).

45) Joan C. Laszcz, Reference Librarian, Euclid Public Library to Jay Ladd, Columbus, June 14, 1976.

46) Hellmut Lehmann-Haupt, *The Book in America; A History of the Making, the Selling, and the Collecting of Books in the United States*, New York, Bowker, 1939.

47) Helen B. Lewis, "CPL Runs School Libraries," *Library Journal*, 75 (July 1950).

48) "Library Executive Development Program," *News From The State Library of Ohio*, 84 (August 20, 1968).

49) Harlow Lindley, "Chronology and Roster of the Ohio State Archaeological and Historical Society," *Ohio State Archaeological and Historical Quarterly*, 54 (July–September 1945).

50) "LSCA Grants Under Titles I and III," *News From The State Library of Ohio*, 82 (June 17, 1968).

51) Dorothy V. Martin, "A History of the Library Movement in Ohio to 1850 with a Special Study of Cincinnati's Library Development," M.A. Thesis, Ohio State University, 1935.

52) Kathryn McChesney, "Kent State University School of Library Science," in *Encyclopedia of Library and Information Science*, New York, Marcel Dekker, 1975.

53) Douglas C. McMutrie, *Pioneer Printing in Ohio*, Cincinnati, Printed by Students of the Printing High School, 1943.

54) William J. McSurely, "History of the Library of Miami University," *The Miami Bulletin*, 6 (February 1908).

55) Judith K. Meyers, "A History of the Antioch College Library, 1850–1929," M.A. Thesis, Kent State University, 1963.

56) Edward A. Miller, *The History of Educational Legislation in Ohio from 1803 to 1850*, Chicago, University of Chicago, 1920.

57) "Month at Random," *Wilson Bulletin*, 12 (March 1938).

58) Minnie S. Monti, "Publishing and Bookselling in Cleveland," *Library Journal*, 75 (July 1950).

59) Josephine Moss, Reference Librarian, William Howard Doane Library to Jay Ladd, Columbus, December 7, 1971.

60) Frank L. Mott, *A History of American Magazines*, 1850–1965, Cambridge, Harvard University Press, 1938.

61) Herbert F. Mutschler, "The Ohio Public Library and State Aid," M.S. Thesis, Western Reserve University, 1952.

62) Paul A.T. Noon, "The Ohio State Library—A Six Year Picture," *Library Journal*, 65 (May 15, 1940).

63) Ohio College Library Center, *Annual Report, 1967/68*, Columbus, 1968.

64) "An Ohio First," *News From the State Library of Ohio*, 54 (March 17, 1966).

65) "Ohio Librarians Found Library Foundation," *Library Journal*, 88 (June 15, 1963).

66) Ohio Library Association, College and University Section, *Regional List of Serials in the College and University Libraries in Ohio*, Ann Arbor, Edwards Brothers, 1936.

67) Ohio Library Association, *News Bulletin*, 1 (April 1931).

68) Ohio Library Association, *Ohio Library Trustees Association, Handbook*, 1968, Columbus, Ohio Library Foundation, 1968.

69) Ohio Library Association, Ohio Library Trustees Association, Steering Committee, *The Ohio Library Development Program*, Ohio Library Association, 1974.

70) Ohio Library Association, *Recommended Job Classifications and Salary Goals for Ohio Academic, Public, School Libraries for 1974–75*, Columbus, 1974.

71) Ohio Library Commission, *Sketches of Ohio Libraries*, Columbus, Fred J. Heer, 1902.

72) Ohio State Teachers' Association, *A History of Education in the State of Ohio*, Columbus, Gazette Printing House, 1876.

73) "Ohio's Books Jobs Program," *American Library Association Bulletin*, 62, (April 1968).

74) "O.S.U. Interlibrary Cooperation Institute Looks to the Future," *News From the State Library of Ohio*, 167, (November 24, 1975).

75) Wyman W. Parker, *Possibility of Extensive Academic Library Cooperation in Ohio; A Survey*, n.p., Ohio College Association.

76) A. Chapman Parsons, "Chap Notes," *Ohio Library Association BULLETIN*, 46 (April 1976).

77) Wanda E. Petty, "The History of the Ohio Penitentiary Library," M.S. Thesis, Western Reserve University, 1949.

78) William J. Rhees, *Manual of Public Libraries, Institutions, and Societies in the United States and British Provinces of North America*, Philadelphia, J.B. Lippincott, 1859.

79) A. Robert Rogers, "Ohio Library Association," Kent, July 1975 (Typewritten).

80) Mildred Sandoe, *County Library Primer*, New York, H.W. Wilson, 1942.

81) Samuel H. Saviers, "The Literary Societies and Their Libraries at Hiram College," M.A. Thesis, Kent State University, 1958.

82) Ronald J. Schink, "A History of the Youngstown University and Its Library," M.S. Thesis, Western Reserve University, 1956.

83) "Senate Bill 262 Becomes Effective November 25," *News From the State Library of Ohio*, 97 (September 22, 1969).

84) Gladys Sepin, "to ALL OLAS ..." *Ohio Library Association BULLETIN*, 26 (September 1956).

85) Kay L. Shaffer, "Annual Report of the Inter-University Library Council Reference and Interlibrary Loan Service, July 1970," (Typewritten).

86) Jesse H. Shera, "Case Western Reserve University," in *Encyclopedia of Library and Information Science*, New York, Marcel Dekker, 1970.

87) John B. Shotwell, *A History of the Schools of Cincinnati*, Cincinnati, The School Life Company, 1902.

88) Jacqueline D. Sisson, *Cooperative System of Ohio Art Libraries*, Columbus, Ohio State University Libraries, 1969.

89) James E. Skipper, "The Ohio State University Library, 1873–1913," Ph.D. Dissertation, University of Michigan, 1960.

90) Claudine M. Smith, "After the Governor's Conference," *Ohio Library Association BULLETIN*, 44 (April 1974)

91) George F. Smythe, *Kenyon College; Its First Century*, New Haven, Yale University Press, 1924.

92) Special Libraries Association, *Special Library Resources*, New York, 1941.

93) Francis R. St. John, *Survey of Library Service for the Blind*, 1956, New York, American Foundation for the Blind, 1957.

94) "State Library Board," *News From the State Library of Ohio*, 157 (December 23, 1974).

95) "Statewide Loan and Solmac," *News From the State Library of Ohio*, 149 (April 16, 1974).

96) Frederick D. Stocker, *Financing Public Libraries in Ohio*, Columbus, Ohio Library Foundation, 1971.

97) Walter Sutton, *The Western Book Trade: Cincinnati as a Nineteenth-Century Publishing and Book-Trade Center*, Columbus, Ohio State University Press, 1961.

98) *Systematic Catalogue of Books Belonging to the Circulating Library Society of Cincinnati: To Which are Prefixed an Historical Preface, The Act of Incorporation and ByLaws, of the Society*, Cincinnati, Looker, Palmer and Reynolds, 1816.

99) Marie E. Szkudlarek, "Historical Development of Work with Children in the Toledo Public Library," M.S. Thesis, Western Reserve University, 1954.

100) L.W. Teeter, "A Brief History of the Growth and Development of the Youngstown Library Association, Youngstown, Ohio," M.A. Thesis, Kent State University, 1956.

101) Virginia Tiefel, "What is ALAO Anyway?" *Ohio Library Association BULLETIN*, 44 (July 1974).

102) "Trade News," *Publishers Weekly*, 209 (May 24, 1976).

103) Jeannie S. Tucker, "Oberlin College Library, 1833–1885," M.S. Thesis, Western Reserve University, 1953.

104) "TWXIL," *News From the State Library of Ohio*, 149 (April 16, 1974).

105) *Union Bibliography of Ohio Printed State Documents, 1803–1970*, Columbus, Ohio Historical Society, 1973.

106) U.S. Department of Education, *Public Libraries in the United States of America; Their History, Condition, and Management*, Washington, Government Printing Office, 1876.

107) W.H. Venable, *Beginnings of Literary Culture in the Ohio Valley*, Cincinnati, Robert Clarke, 1891.

108) Rose L. Vormelker, "Special Libraries at Work," *Library Journal*, 75 (July 1950).

109) Muriel H. Walker, "The Library of the Western Reserve Historical Society," M.A. Thesis, Kent State University, 1952.

110) Caroline P. Ward, "History of the Worthington Public Library," Worthington, n.d.

111) John M. Weller, "160 Years of Library Service to Cincinnati and Hamilton County," in *Contributions to Mid-West Library History*, Ann Arbor, Edwards Brothers, 1964.

112) Norman P. Wetzel, "Mary P. Martin and the Canton Public Library, 1884–1928, A Study in Library Leadership," M.A. Thesis, Kent State University, 1969.

113) Hilda Wick, Head Reference Department, Ohio Wesleyan University to Jay Ladd, December 19, 1971.

114) William L. Williamson, *William Frederick Poole and the Modern Library Movement*, New York, Columbia University Press, 1963.

115) Gertrude Wulfekoetter, "Libraries in Cincinnati," *Library Journal*, 65 (May 15, 1940).

116) Mary Jo Young, "The Akron Public Library, 1942–1957," M.S. Thesis, Western Reserve University, 1958.

Model Library Histories

In 2000, the Ohio Library Council asked public libraries across the state to submit sample histories of their library. Several are listed here as models for anyone faced with the task of writing a library history. This list includes manuscripts, special-occasion booklets, and full-scale books. Copies should be available from the referenced library.

Books

Albright, Margaret and the Reference Department. *Rodman Public Library, A History: 1900–2000*. [Alliance]: Rodman Public Library, 2000.

Cramer, C.H. Open Shelves and *Open Minds: A History of the Cleveland Public Library*. Cleveland: Case Western Reserve University, 1972.

Faries, Elizabeth. *A Century of Service: History of the Dayton Public Library, Dayton, Ohio, 1847–1947*. Rev. ed. Dayton: Dayton Public Library, 1948.

Kelly, Marion H. *More Than Just Books: A History of Cleveland Heights-University Heights Public Library*. Friends of the Cleveland Heights-University Heights Public Library, Inc., 1979.

Noel, David M. *Information Revolution: The History of the Toledo-Lucas County Public Library, 1838–2001*. Virginia Beach: Donning Co. Publishers, 2001.

Booklets

Archbold Community Library: 1916–1995. Nov. 12, 1995.

Novak, Mary Spencer. *Kingsville Library: 1885–2000*. July 2000.

Shaw, Amy, Linda Litzinger, and Frances Black. *History of Southwest Public Libraries, 1891–1991*. 1991.

Telew, Darmar. *They Loved to Read: Massillon Public Library, 100 Years, 1899–1999*. Nov. 1999.

Manuscripts

Brewer, Patricia. "Middletown Public Library to 1975." Sept. 1987.

Daniel, Robert L. "Early Athens Libraries." Paper presented at the Athens Public Library, April 15, 1997.

Erickson, Marsha. "History of Blanchester Public Library." May 1985.

Gambol, Shawna. "History of Harbor Topky Memorial Public Library." [Ashtabula]: Nov. 1997, rev. June, 2000.

Hagloch, Susan B. "History of the Tuscarawas County Public Library." [1999].

Jones, Diane Zuro. "A History of Coshocton Public Library, 1872–1992: A Public Library/Museum Partnership." Master's research paper, Kent State University, May 1993.

Kosman, Jr., George O. "The History of the Fairport Harbor Library." June 1960.

Lockman, Miriam. "History of Arcanum Public Library." 1984.

Martino, Jr., William Daniel. "The History of the Minerva Public Library." Master's thesis, Kent State University, Dec. 1998.

Pancero, Claire. "A Look at the History of the Public Library of Cincinnati and Hamilton County, Especially Its Branches." July 1982.

Somerville, Sally Gearhart. "A brief history of the Public Libraries of Mentor, Ohio." Master's thesis. Kent State University, 1962.

Vano, Leslie J. "The History of the Geauga County Public Library." Paper submitted to the School of Library and Information Science, Kent State University, May 6, 1997.

Bibliography

Americans with Disabilities Act of 1990; Law and Exploration. Chicago: Commerce Clearing House, Inc., 1990.

Armentrout, Mary Ellen. *Carnegie Libraries of Ohio*. Wellington, Ohio: Author, 2003.

Atwater, Caleb. *A History of the State of Ohio, Natural and Civil*. Cincinnati: Glezen & Shepard, [1838].

Blasingame, Ralph. *Survey of Ohio Libraries and State Library Services*. Columbus, State Library of Ohio: 1968.

Carnegie, Andrew. *Autobiography*. Boston: Houghton Mifflin Co.,1920.

Center for the *Study of Librarianship, School of Library and Information Science*, Kent State University. Study of Library Human Resources in Ohio Libraries. Kent, Ohio: The Center, 1991.

Children's Services Task Force. *A Survey of Children's Services in Ohio Public Libraries*. Columbus: Ohio Library Association, 1979.

Cleveland Heights-University Heights Public Library. Annual Reports, 1985–2000.

CNN.com, *www.cnn.com/2000/books/news/08/07/amish.book mobile.ap/*.

Columbus Metropolitan Library Website, *www.cml.lib.oh.us/new/metromouse.cfm*.

Contreras, Sarah A. "Norwalk (Ohio) Public Library: An Historical Overview from 1866 to 1994" (Master's thesis), 1994.

Cramer, C.H. *Open Shelves and Open Minds: A History of the Cleveland Public Library*. Cleveland: Press of Case Western Reserve University, 1972.

Cutler, Sarah J. "The Coonskin Library." *Ohio Archeological and Historical Publications* vol. 26, no. 1 (January 1917).

Cuyahoga County Public Library. *Challenging Age: Library Services for an Aging Population*. Cleveland: Cuyahoga County Public Library, 1989.

Danford, Ardath. "The Metropolitan Library 2002." *Ohio Library Association BULLITEN*, October 1982.

Ditzion, Sidney Herbert. *Arsenals of a Democratic Culture*. Chicago: American Library Association, 1947.

Faries, Elizabeth. "The History of Libraries in Ohio." *Ohio Library Association BULLITEN*, April, 1961.

Fleishman, John. *Free & Public: One Hundred and Fifty Years at the Public Library of Cincinnati and Hamilton County, 1853–2003*. Cincinnati: Orange Frazer Press, 2003.

Galbreath, Charles B. *History of Ohio*. Chicago: American Historical Society, 1925.

Garraty, John A. *A Short History of the American Nation*, 3rd ed. New York: Harper & Row, 1981.

History of Bellaire (Ohio) Public Library. 2000.

Howe, Henry. *Historical Collections of Ohio*. Cincinnati: Derby, Bradley & Co., 1847.

"Internet Access by Library Card." *Cleveland Plain Dealer*, Oct. 28, 1996.

Jones, Theodore. *Carnegie Libraries across America: A Public Legacy.* New York: John Wiley & Sons, Inc., 1997.

Kent, Zachary. *Andrew Carnegie: Steel King and Friend to Libraries.* Springfield, N.J.: Enslow Publishers, 1999.

Lester, Robert M. *Forty Years of Carnegie Giving.* New York: Charles Scribner's Sons, 1941.

Library Builders. London, Eng.: Academy Group Ltd., 1997.

Library Journal, Vol. 6, No. 20 (December 2001).

Livesay, Harold C. *Andrew Carnegie and the Rise of Big Business.* Edited by Oscar Handlin. Boston and Toronto: Little, Brown & Company, 1975.

Lorain Library History, *www.lorain.lib.oh.us/library_history.html.*

MacLeish, Archibald. "Libraries in the Contemporary Crisis." Address at Carnegie Institute, Pittsburgh, Pa. U.S. Government Printing Office, 1939.

Marietta College Archives, special collection of Dawes Memorial Library, Marietta College.

Meltzer, Milton. *The Many Lives of Andrew Carnegie.* Milton Meltzer, 1997.

Murray, Lynda and Susan Hagloch. "Library Funding: Past, Present and Future." Manuscript, 2002.

Nelson, Rachel Wayne. "The Medium-sized Library in the Year 2002." *Ohio Library Association Bulletin,* October 1982.

"First Library in Ohio," *Ohio Library Association Bulletin,* October 1976.

Oehlerts, Donald E. *Books and Blueprints: Building America's Public Libraries*. New York: Greenwood Press, 1991.

Ohio Libraries, Winter 2002.

Ohio Library Council. *Friends Across Ohio*. Columbus: Ohio Library Council, 1996.

Ohio Long Range Program for Improvement of Library Services. Columbus, Ohio: The State Library Board, 1979.

"Ohio's Small Public Library, 2002 A.D." *Ohio Library Association BULLITEN*, October 1982.

Pancero, Claire. "A Look at the History of the Public Library of Cincinnati and Hamilton County." Manuscript, 1982.

Phillips, John. Bookmobile Research. Columbus: Manuscript, 2002.

Pioneer Association of Athens County. *Memorial and History of the Western Library Association.* [Cincinnati], 1982.

Shawan, J.A. "The Public Library in Ohio." *Sketches of Ohio Libraries*, compiled by C.B. Galbreath. Columbus: Fred J. Herr, 1902.

Shubert, Joseph F. Libraries and a Civil Society. Address to the Torch Club of Albany, N.Y., January 7, 2002.

Smith, Claudine. "Books for People: 1817–1967." *The Wonderful World of Ohio* 31 (Dec. 1967): 22–27.

State Library of Ohio. *The Challenge of Library Services to the Aging: Meeting the Current and Future Needs of Older Adults.* Columbus: State Library of Ohio, 1986.

State Library of Ohio. "Federal Funds to Ohio Libraries." Columbus, State Library of Ohio: 1990.

State Library of Ohio. *Institution Library Perspectives*. Columbus: State Library of Ohio, 1977.

State Library of Ohio. Statistical Reports on LSCA Funding, 1965–1974, 1984–1993, and 1994–1998.

U.S. Department of Commerce. *Historical Statistics of the United States, 1789–1945*. Washington, D.C.: U.S. Dept. of Commerce, Bureau of the Census, 1954.

Van Slyck, Abigail Ayres. *Free to All: Carnegie Libraries and American Culture*. University of Chicago Press, 1995.

Wall, Joseph Frazier. *Andrew Carnegie*. Pittsburgh: University of Pittsburgh Press, 1989.

Williams, H.Z. *History of Washington County, Ohio*. Cleveland: H.Z. Williams & Bro., 1881.

Author Biographies

MARGARET ALBRIGHT, a graduate of Loyola University in New Orleans, has worked for the last five years in Rodman Public Library's Reference Department. She indexes and maintains materials relating to the history of Alliance and was the author/editor of the library's centennial history book.

HARRIET CLEM is director of the Rodman Public Library in Alliance, a post she has held since 1969. She began her library career by learning to drive a bookmobile. In the Ohio Library Council she has chaired divisions and committees and was a "founding Mother of the Library Accounting Division." In the Alliance community she has served twice as the president of the Chamber of Commerce and is active in several organizations.

JEFF FRENCH, Deputy Director, Euclid Public Library. B.A. Cleveland State University, M.L.S. Kent State University. Member and past chair of the Ohio Library Council Intellectual Freedom Committee.

ALAN HALL, Native of Marietta, Ohio, and has worked in Ohio's public libraries for thirty-three years. For the past twenty years, he has been the director of the Public Library of Steubenville and Jefferson County in Steubenville, Ohio.

STEPHEN HEDGES holds a Master of Library and Information Science degree from the University of South Carolina and a Ph.D. in the History and Theory of Music from The University of Chicago. He is a lifelong resident of Athens County, Ohio, and has served as the director of the Nelsonville Public Library since 1997.

MELINDA HILL is a freelance writer and editor currently making her home in Washington, D.C., where she will begin work on a Master of the Arts in Religion at Catholic University in Fall 2003. She grew up in Ohio, and in Ohio libraries, and recently served as the Stack Manager of the Fairborn Branch of Greene County Public Library.

CINDY LOMBARDO is director of the Orrville Public Library. She holds a doctorate in education from The Ohio State University and a master's degree in library science from Kent State University. Cindy has served on numerous ALA selection committees including Best Books for Young Adults, Popular Paperbacks for Young Adults, Michael Printz, Caldecott, Carnegie, Mildred Batchelder, and Notable Recordings. She is a current board member of the Ohio Library Council and the Cleveland Area Metropolitan System. Cindy is also the editor of *Capturing Community* (2002), *Capturing Character* (2003), and a contributor to *The World Through Children's Books* (2002).

DAVID C. MILLER is editor of the *Sentinel-Tribune* in Bowling Green. He is a member and former president of the State Library of Ohio Board and a past chairman of the Ohio Library Council and the Ohio Library Trustee Association. The author of "Focus on Trustees" column in the Rural Library Services Newsletter since 1994, he was named the Ohio Public Library Trustee of the Year in 1995.

Author Biographies

RACHEL WAYNE NELSON has served the Ohio library community as the editor of the Ohio Library Association Bulletin, as president of the Ohio Library Association, and as director of the Cleveland Heights-University Heights Public Library. She was inducted into the Ohio Library Council Hall of Fame in 1995.

H. BAIRD TENNEY, co-author of the buildings section of this volume, has served as a trustee in several library groups, starting with his own area—Cleveland Heights-University Heights. Subsequently he was a board member of the State Library of Ohio, the Ohio Library Foundation, and finally a founding member of OPLIN (the Ohio Public Library Information Network). He was elected to the Ohio Library Trustees Hall of Fame in 1997. Tenney's background is in business and industry. He served aboard a Navy destroyer in the early post-WWII era.

STEVE WOOD has been with the Cleveland Heights-University Heights Public Library for twenty-five years most recently as its director. He is active with the Ohio Library Council and was named Librarian of the Year in 1998.